Berlitz®

Sri Lanka

Front cover: south
coast beach

Right: traditional masks

TOP 10 ATTRACTIONS

Pinnewala Elephant Orphanage Home to the world's largest collection of captive elephants *(page 52)*

Sigiriya A spectacular, ancient citadel featuring the 'Sigiriya Damsels' *(page 65)*

Buddhas of Polonnaruwa • Explore the impressive, ancient sculptures and carvings in this ruined city *(page 67)*

Galle Fort A perfectly preserved colonial time capsule *(page 37)*

Temple of the Tooth Home to Sri Lanka's most venerated religious relic on Kandy Lake *(page 48)*

Bentota The west coast's premier beach destination *(page 33)*

Yala National Park Famous for its significant leopard population *(page 44)*

Horton Plains National Park and World's End See some of Sri Lanka's finest scenery, and most magnificent views *(page 57)*

Adam's Peak See dawn's shadow cast from revered Adam's Peak *(page 59)*

Anuradhapura Home to an astonishing collection of impressive stupas *(page 74)*

A PERFECT TOUR

Days 1–3   Temples

Pick up a car and driver for your tour and head northeast to Sri Lanka's Cultural Triangle. Spend a day cycling around the ruined city of Polonnaruwa and a second day visiting the magical cave temples of Dambulla and the rock-top citadel of Sigiriya, with an elephant safari at Minneriya or Kaudulla National Parks on one of the three days.

Day 7   Time for tea

Travel south through the hills to Nuwara Eliya, stopping for a visit to the tea factory and plantation at Labookelie en route. Spend the afternoon exploring Nuwara Eliya, strolling through Victoria Park and then taking afternoon tea on the terrace at the Grand Hotel. Round off the day with dinner at the town's wonderfully time-warped Hill Club.

Day 8   Views aplenty

Continue south to Horton Plains National Park, making the enjoyable walk around the park (a few hours) with its beautiful stands of cloudforest, and sensational views over the lowlands below from the escarpment at World's End. Continue on to idyllic Ella, one of the island's prettiest villages.

Days 4–6   Culture in Kandy

Head south to Kandy, Sri Lanka's cultural capital, and explore the temples and palaces, as well as the Peradeniya Botanical Gardens and Pinnewala Elephant Orphanage. Attend an early morning puja at the Temple of the Tooth, and take in a nightly performance of the traditional, acrobatic Kandyan dancing.

OF SRI LANKA

Day 10 Buddhas and big cats

Spend the morning driving south from Ella via the spectacular Rawana Ella Falls and the majestic Buddha statues at Buduruwagala – an inspiring sequence of seven figures carved in low relief into the looming rock face. Then while away the afternoon looking for leopards in Yala National Park, Sri Lanka's most popular park and home to one of the world's densest concentrations of these felines.

Day 14 Colombo

Loop back around the coastal road and finish your tour with a visit to Colombo, being sure to visit the vibrant bazaar district of the Pettah and the fine National Museum. Make some time for last-minute shopping in one of the city's fine boutiques and a meal at one of its excellent Sri Lankan or Indian restaurants before flying home.

Day 9 Around Ella

Spend the day exploring the beautiful countryside around Ella, an English-style village oozing charm, making either the short but rewarding walk up Little Adam's Peak, or the longer hike to the summit of Ella Rock.

Days 11–13 Beach time

Crash out on one of the idyllic beaches fringing the west and south coasts, such as at Bentota – also the island's water sports capital – backpacker-friendly Unawatuna, or Mirissa, enjoying a stay at one of the superb hotels or villas listed on pages 133–42.

CONTENTS

37

65

74

39

57

47

INTRODUCTION

Poised a few degrees above the equator amidst the azure waters of the Indian Ocean, Sri Lanka is, for many visitors, one of Asia's ultimate tropical island paradises. Medieval traders and modern tourists alike have been beguiled by the island's endless golden beaches and abundant natural riches, from cinnamon to sapphires and elephants. Marco Polo declared it the finest island of its size in the world, while generations of other travellers, from Ibn Battuta to Mark Twain, have waxed lyrical over the country's natural beauty and palm-fringed shores.

The tropical island stereotypes are only part of the truth, however. Although a relatively small nation by Asian standards, Sri Lanka has tremendous physical, cultural and ethnic diversity, as well as a long and distinguished history stretching far back into the pre-Christian era. As the home of one of the world's oldest and purest Buddhist traditions, Sri Lanka boasts a unique and distinctive cultural character, while the island's wide range of landscapes, from tropical beaches to misty upland tea plantations, lends it an extraordinary scenic appeal.

The Modern Nation

The Democratic Socialist Republic of Sri Lanka (as it has been known since 1972, when it ditched the old British colonial name of Ceylon) now boasts a population of over 20 million, and is growing rapidly. Almost three-quarters of the population are Buddhist Sinhalese, the descendants of settlers from North India, but there are also significant numbers of South Indian-descended Hindu Tamils, par-

The coastline at Galle

ticularly in the north and east of the island. The nation's two main languages are Sinhala (the language of the Sinhalese) and Tamil, while English is also widely spoken. The island has been a multi-party democracy since independence in 1948.

Sri Lanka's recent history has been overshadowed by the civil war between the Sri Lankan government and the separatist Tamil Tigers (LTTE), which ravaged the island from the early 1980s through to the beginning of 2009, when the Sri Lankan Army finally succeeded in destroying the last remnants of LTTE power. The island was also devas-

The Many Names of Sri Lanka

Sri Lanka has had many names over the centuries. The island's ancient Sanskrit name was Sinhaladvipa, 'Lion Island', named after the Sinhalese themselves, and it was this name which provided the basis for most of the island's subsequent appellations. In Pali, the classic language of early Buddhism, Sinhala is 'Sihalam', pronounced 'Silam', which was subsequently bastardised by the Portuguese into Ceilão, by the Dutch to Zeylan, and by the British to Ceylon. Early Arab traders, meanwhile, transformed it into Serendib, the origin of the English word 'serendipity', signifying the making of happy discoveries by chance, a word which is still much used to describe Sri Lanka's fortuitous pleasures.

Not that these were the island's only names. The island was also known in ancient Sanskrit literature as Ratnadvipa ('Island of Gems'), while the Greeks and Romans knew it as Taprobane, a mutation of another ancient Sanskrit name for the island, Tambapanni ('copper-coloured'), derived from the colour of the beach on which Prince Vijaya first landed. For the Sinhalese, however, the island has always been Lanka – as it is called in the great Indian epic the *Ramayana* – and it was to this name, with the additional 'Sri', meaning 'resplendent' or 'auspicious', that the nation's name officially reverted in 1972.

tated by the 2004 Asian
tsunami, which killed al-
most 40,000 people in Sri
Lanka alone and reduced
much of the seaboard to
ruins. However, subsequent
reconstruction of coastal
tourist areas has been swift
and thorough, and the is-
land's tourist facilities are
now of a higher standard
than ever before, reflecting
the industry's increasingly
crucial role in the national
economy.

Waterfall in the hill country

Landscapes

One of Sri Lanka's greatest attractions is the remarkable
range of landscapes that are packed into the island's modest
dimensions. It is possible to wake up sweating on the coast
and then be shivering by lunchtime in the breezy heights of
the hill country, just a few hours' drive away. Most of the island's 1,340km (830 miles) of coastline is fringed with idyllic golden-sand beaches, many of which remain remarkably
undeveloped, offering a perfect tropical bolthole for those
wishing to escape the commercialisation that has overtaken
many other parts of Asia.

Away from the sultry coast lies a world of scenic contrasts,
from the rugged mountains and misty green uplands of the
hill country to the rolling, wildlife-rich savannahs of the
north and east. Thorny dry monsoon forest carpets much of
the lowland plains, while tea plantations blanket the hills,
dotted with perfectly preserved pockets of rainforest and
cloudforest. This physical variety in turn supports a unique-

ly varied array of flora and fauna, including thousands of wild elephants, one of the world's largest leopard populations, and a vast number of bird species, many of which are found only on the island.

One Island, Many People

The island's physical diversity is mirrored by its cosmopolitan cultural make-up, the legacy of centuries of commerce and conquest experienced by Sri Lanka thanks to its strategic position on the trade routes of the Indian Ocean. Foremost amongst the island's myriad ethnic groups are the Sinhalese, originally from North India, who arrived in Sri Lanka sometime around the 4th or 5th century BC. The Sinhalese now make up over two-thirds of the population and have given the country its rich Buddhist traditions and a religious outlook that continues to shape the nation.

Boy monks at Nuwara Eliya

Tamils from South India, who have probably been in Sri Lanka as long as the Sinhalese, make up the island's second-largest ethnic group and have created a vibrant local Hindu culture which runs parallel to the Buddhist majority.

Waves of Arab, Indian and Malay traders and Portuguese, Dutch and British settlers have also left their mark on everything from the island's cooking and architecture to its religion, railways and economy.

Some sense of Sri Lanka's cultural diversity can be gleaned by comparing the contrasting lifestyles of two of its smallest but most distinctive ethnic groups. In Colombo, the urbane Burghers – white, English-speaking Sri Lankans of mixed European descent – still play a leading role in the island's cultural life. In the remote jungles of the east, a handful of aboriginal Veddahs, the island's oldest inhabitants, who have lived here for at least 18,000 years, continue to pursue their traditional hunter-gatherer existence.

Buddhas and Beaches

The Sinhalese civilisation can be traced back to the 3rd century BC, when Buddhism first arrived on here. By the 1st century AD the great city of Anuradhapura had developed into a vibrant centre of Buddhist learning, its sizeable population of monks supported by the immense irrigation works with which the early Sinhalese transformed the island's arid northern plains into a fertile rice bowl. The remains of this early Sinhalese civilisation, found at Anuradhapura, Sigiriya and Polonnaruwa, include an astonishing array of monasteries, shrines, statues and vast stupas, the largest man-made structures in the ancient world, bar the two largest Egyptian pyramids.

Sri Lanka's other attractions are legion, from the atmospheric tea plantations of the hill country to the vibrant cultural traditions of Kandy and the more contemporary urban attractions of Colombo. It is now also possible to strike off into the north or east of the island, only recently reopened to casual visitors after the bloody end to the civil war in 2009 (although it's best to double-check the latest security situation before deciding whether to travel to these areas). If none of the above appeal, you can always simply go and lie on a beach.

A BRIEF HISTORY

Sri Lanka's past is as long as it is varied, with a recorded history stretching back many centuries before the birth of Christ. This is one of the world's oldest Buddhist strongholds, but also a cosmopolitan melting pot of assorted Asian and European adventurers, traders and settlers, many of whom have left a lasting mark on the island's religion, culture and cuisines.

Prehistory

Early archaeological evidence of human settlement in Sri Lanka remains slight. The first people to arrive on the island were the Veddahs, an aboriginal hunter-gatherer people thought to be related to the aboriginal peoples of Australia, Malaysia and the Nicobar Islands. They are believed to have arrived in Sri Lanka by around 16,000BC, or possibly much earlier, and survive in isolated pockets in the east of the island in ever-diminishing numbers.

Starting around the 5th century BC, waves of settlers began to arrive in Sri Lanka from northern India. The first arrivals are thought to have come from modern Gujarat, and were followed by further immigrants from Orissa and Bengal. These people, the ancestors of the modern Sinhalese, initially settled on the west coast and gradually pushed inland towards the centre of the northern plains where, in around 377BC, they established the settlement of Anuradhapura. This was Sri Lanka's first great city and remained the focus of the island's history for almost 1,500 years.

The Anuradhapura Period

The first major landmark in the development of Anuradhapura was the arrival of Buddhism in 246BC, brought to the island by Mahinda, the son of the great Indian Buddhist emperor Asoka. Mahinda quickly converted the Sinhalese king, Devanampiya Tissa, who embraced the new faith enthusiastically. Buddhism provided the Sinhalese with an important sense of national identity, and Anuradhapura soon developed a markedly religious emphasis with the establishment of the great Mahavihara monastery and other Buddhist institutions.

Ruvanvalisaya stupa at Anuradhapura

Soon after Devanampiya Tissa's death, however, Anuradhapura suffered the first of the invasions by Tamils from south India which were to prove a recurrent feature of its entire history. The Tamil general Elara ruled for 44 years before the famous warrior-king Dutugemunu succeeded in ousting the Tamils, uniting the entire island under Sinhalese rule for the first time.

The subsequent history of Anuradhapura repeated the theme thus established, with periods of relative stability interspersed with chaotic intervals during which Tamil invaders and Sinhalese infighting threw the island into disarray. In AD473, for example, the notorious Kassapa murdered his father, King Dhatusena, and briefly established a rival capital at Sigiriya. Despite these periodic upheavals, Anuradhapura developed into one of the great cities of its age. Huge tracts of the arid surrounding plains were irrigated and vast reservoirs were built *(see page 76)*, while the city's great monasteries served as bastions of the Buddhist faith and learning. During the 9th and 10th centuries, however, repeated Tamil invasions slowly brought Anuradhapura to its knees, until in 993 the army of the Chola king Rajaraja sacked the city, an event from which it never recovered.

Polonnaruwa Period

Having reduced Anuradhapura to rubble, the Cholas established a new capital at the city of Polonnaruwa. The site had the great strategic advantage of being further from India, and thus less vulnerable to foreign interference, and the Cholas ruled there for 75 years until they were toppled by another great Sinhalese warrior-king, Vijayabahu. Vijayabahu's reconquest of Polonnaruwa ushered in a final golden age of

Buddha at Polonnaruwa – a golden age of Sinhalese culture

Sinhalese culture in the north. His successor, Parakramabahu, transformed the city into one of the finest of its age, and a rival to the abandoned Anuradhapura. Once again, however, Tamil invaders were to prove the Sinhalese capital's undoing. In 1212 a new wave of Pandyan invaders arrived, and in 1215 the infamous Magha seized control of Polonnaruwa. His chaotic reign of terror left the city crippled, the monasteries shattered and the great irrigation systems of the north in chronic disrepair, signalling the end of the great early Sinhalese civilisations of northern Sri Lanka.

Sinhalese Decline and the Rise of Jaffna

As Polonnaruwa crumbled, so the Sinhalese nobility gradually migrated south towards the relative safety of the hill country, establishing a series of transient capitals whose kings enjoyed increasingly limited control over the island as a whole. Over the next two centuries the island's great Buddhist institutions collapsed, whilst Tamil Hindu influence began to permeate the island's culture and religion. At the same time, yet another wave of Tamil invaders established a vibrant new kingdom centred on the city of Jaffna, at the northernmost point of the island, from where they gradually pushed south and east, establishing the Tamil–Sinhalese cultural divide which endures to this day.

The Portuguese

By the beginning of the 16th century, the remnants of the Sinhalese aristocracy had established two major rival centres of power: one in the hills at Kandy, and another near the coast at Kotte, near present-day Colombo. It was the Kingdom of Kotte which was the first to experience the depredations of a new and more exotic wave of invaders, the Portuguese. The Portuguese arrived in 1505 in search of spices, and soon established a fort at Colombo (the origin of

Entrance to Dutch-built Fort Frederick, Trincomalee

the modern city), from where they engaged in periodic skirmishes with Kotte. Although the Sinhalese were initially able to resist Portuguese attacks on land, they had no response to the Europeans' sea power. The Portuguese gradually spread out along the coast, annexing the declining Kingdom of Jaffna in 1619 and fighting their way around the seaboard until they had established control over much of the island's lowlands, taking over the Sinhalese king's monopoly on the sale of elephants, as well as the lucrative trade in spices such as pepper and betel nut. The Portuguese invasion was accompanied by a fervent campaign of missionary activity, with considerable swathes of the coastal population converted to Catholicism and numerous temples destroyed. This explains the origin of the numerous Sri Lankan de Silvas, Pereiras and Fernandos whose names fill the island's telephone directories to this day.

The Kandyan Kingdom and the Dutch

One final bastion of Sinhalese power remained, however: the Kingdom of Kandy, buried deep in the impenetrable hills of the interior. The Portuguese were unable to subdue Kandy, despite repeated attempts – while the Kandyans, in turn, launched offensives against the Portuguese, though their lack of sea power prevented them from permanently evicting the European interlopers.

It was the hope of driving the Portuguese out of Sri Lanka once and for all that led the Kandyans into an unlikely alliance with another European power, the Dutch, who had increasingly begun to covet the island's rich natural resources.

Between 1638 and 1658 the Dutch systematically attacked and overran Portuguese coastal strongholds, though they showed no signs of handing any of these conquered territories back to the Kandyans. Having established their mastery over much of the island, the pragmatic Dutch set about promoting trade and systematically exploiting the island's commercial possibilities. They also made modest efforts to promote their Calvinist Protestant faith at the expense of Catholicism, which they declared illegal.

The British

It was, however, the third and final of the colonial powers to occupy Sri Lanka, the British, who were to exercise the most lasting influence on the island. Like the Dutch, the British (already firmly established in neighbouring India) had had their eyes on Sri Lanka – particularly the strategic deep-water harbour at Trincomalee – for some years. Unlike the Dutch, they were able to take possession of the island with a minimum of military fuss thanks to the Napoleonic Wars in Europe. When the Netherlands fell to the French in 1794, the British stepped in to 'protect' the

A Dutch settlement, 1682

Kerck - huys

Dutch colony from French interference. The Dutch mounted only token resistance, and British possession of the island was formally ratified by the Treaty of Amiens in 1802.

Like the Dutch, British policy in Sri Lanka was largely aimed at maximising the island's commercial potential and their legacies – most notably the country's tea industry, its railways, and the English language itself – remain essential elements of the modern island's commercial and cultural landscape. The British also finally succeeded in taking possession of the recalcitrant Kandyan Kingdom, thanks to the efforts of the arch colonial schemer Sir John D'Oyly, who succeeded in turning the kingdom's Sinhalese nobles against their Tamil king. In 1815, after three centuries of spirited and often bloody resistance, the Kandyans meekly surrendered, finally extinguishing the last bastion of independent native rule in the island.

A European in a rickshaw, 1933

Towards Independence

The later part of the 19th century was a period of intense soul-searching for the Sinhalese. Faced with an occupying and unshiftable European power and the constantly encroaching influence of missionary Christianity, the islanders began to re-evaluate their traditional religious and cultural beliefs, creating a vigorous Buddhist revivalist movement. As the 20th century dawned, this movement became increasingly politicised, leading to the foundation of the Ceylon National Congress in 1919. The British gradually began to make concessions, and in 1931 a new constitution gave the island's political leaders the first opportunity to exercise real (though still limited) political power, as well as granting the islanders universal suffrage.

During World War II Sri Lanka became a strategically vital base for British operations in Asia following the fall of Indonesia, Burma and Singapore to the Japanese. It even attracted the attentions of the Japanese air force, who launched raids against Colombo and Trincomalee. Following the war, the enfeebled British Empire gave up its colonial possessions, and Sri Lanka finally achieved independence on 6 February, 1948.

Independence

Power was handed to the United National Party (UNP), a generally conservative party dominated by the English-educated leaders such as the Senanayake family, who had risen to prominence under the British. The UNP ruled until 1956, when they were ousted by the more populist and nationalist Sri Lanka Freedom Party (SLFP), led by the charismatic S.W.R.D. Bandaranaike. These two parties have alternated in power ever since – with the Senanayake and Bandaranaike families (or their close relatives) providing most of the island's leaders up until recent times. This has

S.W.R.D. Bandaranaike

particularly been the case with the SLFP. When S.W.R.D. Bandaranaike was assassinated by a Buddhist monk in 1959, leadership of the party passed quickly to his widow, Srimavo, who thus became the world's first ever female prime minister. Their daughter, Chandrika Kumaratunga would later serve as both prime minister and president, a dynastic family sequence to rival the Nehrus in India, and one which gained the SLFP the nickname of the 'Sri Lanka Family Party'.

The early years of Independence were kind to Sri Lanka, but during the 1950s and 1960s increasing economic difficulties and falling living standards led to widespread disenchantment, culminating in the 1971 armed rebellion staged by the JVP, a quasi-Marxist, student-led organisation with a pronounced nationalistic, anti-Tamil stance. The insurrection was put down with considerable loss of life, but anti-Tamil rhetoric became a feature of national political life. A controversial sequence of legislative changes drove the Tamils into the margins of the island's commercial and political life. A new generation of militant Tamil organisations sprang up in the north of the island – including the Tamil Tigers, or LTTE – and the number of confrontations between them and the Sri Lankan police and army began to increase.

Civil War

Anti-Tamil sentiment reached a peak in 1983 when, following an LTTE massacre of an army patrol in the north, Sinhalese mobs launched an orgy of violence against Tamils across the island, killing as many as 2,000 people. Thousands of Tamils fled to the north or departed overseas, while corresponding numbers of Sinhalese came south. By 1985 the conflict had developed into an all-out civil war between the Sinhalese-dominated Sri Lankan Army (SLA) and the guerrilla forces of the LTTE.

In 1987 the Indian government, under increasing pressure from its own enormous Tamil population, intervened in the conflict by despatching the hugely controversial Indian Peace-Keeping Force (IPKF) to the island to enforce a ceasefire, although it rapidly became embroiled in heavy fighting with the Tamils it had allegedly come to protect. Meanwhile, in 1987, a second JVP rebellion broke out in the south, reducing the entire island to a state of near anarchy.

The JVP rebellion was once again put down with brutal force, while in 1990 the IPKF, facing mounting casualties, left the island, to the relief of both Tamils and Sinhalese. Heavy fighting continued throughout the north and east between the LTTE and SLA, while repeated LTTE suicide-bomber attacks against Colombo and other southern targets claimed thousands of civilian casualties. A ceasefire was finally agreed in 2002, and the island enjoyed a few years of relative peace, al-

The withdrawal of the Indian Peace-Keeping Force in 1990

though the situation steadily deteriorated, exacerbated by the catastrophic effects of the Asian tsunami, which struck the island on 26 December 2004, killing some 38,000 people and reducing many settlements around the coast to rubble.

Peace at Last?

The military stalemate was finally broken in 2005, with the election as president of Mahinda Rajapakse. In 2007, Rajapakse launched a decisive offensive against the LTTE. Over the next 18 months the SLA systematically drove the Tigers out of their strongholds in the east and then north of the island, finally announcing victory (along with the killing of the LTTE's legendary leader, Velupillai Prabhakaran) in May 2008. The triumph was achieved at a terrible human and economic cost, Alongside accusations of widespread atrocities and war crimes. Rajapakse was elected for a second five-year term in 2010, although human-rights issues continue to cloud his reputation, ranging from the treatment of Tamil civilians through to independent journalists and rival politicians – Rajapakse's opponent in the 2010 elections, General Sarath Fonseka, was subsequently threatened with execution for 'treason' and is currently languishing in prison.

The clock tower at Galle Fort

Historical Landmarks

c.16,000BC Arrival of Veddahs.

c.500BC Arrival of first Sinhalese settlers.

377BC Foundation of Anuradhapura.

247BC King Devanampiya Tissa converts to Buddhism.

161BC Dutugemunu establishes first island-wide Sinhalese kingdom.

AD473 Kassapa establishes short-lived capital at Sigiriya.

993 Cholas establish new capital at Polonnaruwa.

1070 Vijayabahu drives out Cholas and re-establishes Sinhalese rule.

1215 Tamil mercenary Magha seizes control of Polonnaruwa.

13th–15th centuries Series of short-lived Sinhalese capitals, leading to establishment of Kandy and Kotte. Rise of Jaffna kingdom.

1505 Arrival of Portuguese, and establishment of fort in Colombo.

1619 Portuguese annexe Jaffna.

1638 Beginning of Dutch attacks against Portuguese.

1658 Jaffna falls to Dutch; end of Portuguese power in Sri Lanka.

1796 British take control of Sri Lanka from Dutch.

1867 First tea plantation established. Colombo to Kandy railway built.

1919 Foundation of Ceylon National Congress, first nationalist party.

1948 Country achieves independence. Changes name to Sri Lanka.

1959 Prime minister S.W.R.D. Bandaranaike assassinated by a Buddhist monk. His widow becomes the world's first female prime minister.

1971 Armed insurrection against government by JVP.

1972 Country becomes Democratic Socialist Republic of Sri Lanka.

1983 Civil war erupts between government forces and LTTE.

1987 Arrival of Indian Peace-Keeping Force (IPKF) in the north.

1990 Departure of IPKF after failure to keep the peace.

1993 Suicide bomber kills prime minister Ranasinghe Premadasa.

1996 Sri Lanka co-hosts and wins World Cricket Cup.

2004 Tsunami devastates coastal areas of island, killing thousands.

2005 Mahinda Rajapakse elected president.

2008 Final defeat of LTTE by Sri Lankan Army.

2010 Mahinda Rajapakse re-elected president.

WHERE TO GO

A classic Sri Lankan itinerary would include a few days in the Cultural Triangle, a tour through Kandy and the hill country, and a spell spent on the beaches of the southern or western coast. These places offer an overview of the island's contrasting landscapes and complex history, but they are by no means all the country has to offer. Hiring a car and driver *(see page 118)* means you get to see a lot more than you otherwise would, but you still won't get anywhere fast. You will, however, get a feeling for the island's essentially rural lifestyle and sleepy pace of life.

COLOMBO

In a predominantly rural island, **Colombo** is Sri Lanka's one true metropolis. Home to around three million people and most of the island's significant commercial and industrial activity, the city sprawls along the west coast for the best part of 60km (40 miles), an endless straggle of chaotic and traffic-infested suburbs which can seem totally out of scale and character with the rest of the island. Unsurprisingly, this noisy, crowded and disorienting urban morass ranks low on most tourist itineraries, but despite initial impressions, there is plenty in the city's contrasting districts and a handful of low-key sights to merit at least a day's exploration.

Fort and the Pettah

The heart of old Colombo is **Fort** district, first established by the Portuguese, who constructed the now vanished fortifications after which the district is named. Once the centrepiece of Colombo's commercial and administrative life, Fort

A monk at the Gangaramaya Temple in Colombo

Seema Malaka temple by the waters of Beira Lake

bore the brunt of repeated LTTE attacks against Colombo during the civil war, and is now rather forlorn, with a heavy army presence and large areas closed off for security reasons. The heart of the district is marked by the distinctive **Lighthouse Clock Tower**, erected in 1857, while other crumbling relics of 19th-century British enterprise lie dotted around, most notably the famous old **Cargills** department store. At the southern edge of the district rises an incongruous cluster of high-rises containing several five-star hotels and the twin towers of the **World Trade Centre**.

East of Fort stretches Colombo's most absorbing area, the **Pettah**, a crowded and chaotic bazaar district whose tight grid of streets is crammed full of an astonishing number of shops whose owners frantically trade everything from Ayurvedic herbs to mobile phones. At the heart of the district, the **Dutch Period Museum** (Tue–Sat 9am–5pm; charge) houses a modest selection of exhibits relating to

Dutch life in colonial Sri Lanka in an atmospheric old villa. **D**
Just to the north is the **Jami ul-Alfar** mosque, the district's
most eye-catching landmark, its exterior decorated in bright
red and white stripes.

Galle Face Green and Slave Island

South of Fort stretches **Galle Face Green**, bounded to the **E**
north by the high-rises of Fort and the sprawling neoclassi-
cal Government Secretariat, and to the south by the famous
old colonial **Galle Face Hotel**. A favourite city meeting
place, the green really comes alive towards dusk when half
the city descends on it to swap gossip, fly kites, enjoy the sea
breezes and sample the unusual snacks served up by innumerable stalls set up along the promenade.

Heading inland from Galle Face Green, the ramshackle
district of **Slave Island** (named after the African slaves once
corralled here by the Portuguese and Dutch) is home to a
cluster of Hindu and Buddhist shrines, including the city's
two most interesting Buddhist temples. The first is the unusual **Seema Malaka** (designed by Sri Lanka's foremost **F**
20th-century architect, Geoffrey Bawa), whose wooden
buildings occupy three platforms set out over the waters of
Lake Beira – particularly beautiful when illuminated at night.

Just east of here, the more extensive and traditional
Gangaramaya comprises a peaceful courtyard surrounded **G**
by shrines populated by as-
sorted deities, including a
huge modern ceramic Bud-
dha. The quirky attached
museum (charge) displays
thousands of gifts presented
to the temple over the years,
including an unusual collection of vintage cars.

Dutch deterrent

The Dutch discouraged
slaves from attempting to
escape Slave Island by keep-
ing the surrounding canals
and the waters of Beira
Lake populated with a large
number of crocodiles.

Southern Colombo

South of Slave Island, the serene suburb of **Cinnamon Gardens** is the city's smartest address, with leafy roads lined with grand colonial villas and the peaceful **Vihara Mahadevi Park**, which stretches south of the modern town hall. The park is home to the **National Museum** (Sat–Thur 9am–5pm; charge). Occupying one of Colombo's finest colonial buildings, the museum's extensive collection includes some fine ancient Buddhist and Hindu statuary, an excellent selection of *kolam* masks and the lavish regalia of the last king of Kandy.

South of Galle Face Green, southern Colombo's major traffic artery, the smelly and congested Galle Road, strikes due south through the districts of Kollupitiya and Bambalapitiya, now home to many of the city's top shops and restaurants, including the outstanding **Barefoot** shop and the beautiful **Gallery Café** *(see pages 88 and 110–11)*. A few kilometres further south, **Dehiwala Zoo** (daily 8.30am–6pm; charge) is home to a comprehensive collection of international and indigenous wildlife, including a good selection of the island's local fauna, from sloth bears to leopards.

At the southern edge of Colombo, 10km (6 miles) south of Fort, the laid-back suburb of **Mount Lavinia** offers a peaceful respite from the city streets to the north, presided over by the venerable **Mount Lavinia Hotel**, whose graceful white buildings provide the suburb's major landmark. Although it is more popular with locals than with foreign tourists, the stretch of rather grubby beach here – the closest to the city centre – makes it a popular spot, particularly at weekends.

Ten kilometres east of Fort lies the **Kelaniya Raja Maha Vihara**, the most important Buddhist shrine in Colombo. Built to commemorate the third and last of the Buddha's visits to the island, the modern temple complex comprises a vibrant and colourful array of modern paintings and sculptures, and is always lively with pilgrims.

THE WEST COAST

Sri Lanka's west coast is the most developed part of the island, and its innumerable large-scale resort hotels remain the driving force behind the country's sizeable package-tourist industry. Much of the development here has been extensive and unregulated, and if you want unspoiled beaches and a true taste of the island's fabled serenity you will have to head further south. Having said that, the west coast is home to many of Sri Lanka's finest beachside hotels, both large and small, and still offers pockets of tropical charm, if you know where to look.

Negombo and Around

Thirty kilometres (20 miles) north of Colombo, **Negombo** 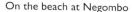 owes its popularity mainly to its proximity to the international airport, offering a convenient first (or last) stop on a tour of

On the beach at Negombo

the island. The wide beach here has a plethora of guesthouses and resort hotels, and although there are far nicer beaches further south, Negombo has enough tropical charm to merit a day's rest and recuperation after a long-haul flight. Tourists share the beach with the local Karava fishermen, whose flotillas of oruwa boats make a memorable sight as they return from offshore fishing trips during the early morning. Ingeniously constructed, an *oruwa* is fashioned from narrow canoes topped by an enormous sail which is kept steady in the water by cantilevered wooden floats. This type of vessel is known in Tamil as *ketti-maran*, the origin of the word 'catamaran'.

South of the resort, **Negombo town** is dominated by the enormous pink bulk of **St Mary's Church**, testament to the town's status as one of the strongholds of Christianity on the west coast. The town was formerly an important Dutch settlement thanks to its strategic control of the lucrative local cin-

Oruwas returning to harbour

namon trade and it preserves a few traces of its colonial heritage, including fragments of an old **Dutch fort**, as well as its old **Dutch canal**, which runs due north along the coast all the way to Puttalam, over 80km (50 miles) away. It is possible to organise **boat trips** along the canal or off the coast in oruwa boats as well as through the wetlands of **Muthurajawela**, south of the town, home to rich bird life and other fauna.

Negombo fish market

Kalutara

Just south of the great urban sprawl of Colombo, **Kalutara** ◀ ❸ has a long stretch of fine, though rather narrow, beach backed by a string of large-scale resort hotels. The lively town itself is worth a visit for the **Gangatilaka Vihara**, a picturesque temple whose enormous stupa looms imposingly over the main coastal road. The stupa also has the unusual distinction of being the only entirely hollow one in the world – step inside to experience the resonant echoes and murals depicting scenes from the Buddha's life.

Beruwala, Bentota and Around

The epicentre of the Sri Lankan package-tourist industry lies further south at the twin resorts of Beruwala and Bentota. **Beruwala** is the most developed resort in the island, with a beautiful wide stretch of fine golden sand flanked by a dense concentration of hotels mainly catering for European sun seekers during the northern winter. South of here, **Bentota** ◀ ❹ has an equally fine swathe of sand, but the atmosphere is more laid-back, with a sequence of fine hotels strung at discreet intervals along the coast. Bentota is also the island's water sports capital, with numerous activities ranging from jet-skiing to windsurfing on the tranquil waters of the **Bentota lagoon**, which meanders inland from here, and also offers a rewarding destination for boat trips into its tangled waterways and mangrove swamps. Both Beruwala and Bentota have a selection of diving schools, as well as the densest concentration of ayurvedic hotels on the island.

Sandwiched between Bentota and Beruwala, the workaday little town of **Aluthgama** is home to a cluster of attractive low-key guesthouses backing the Bentota lagoon, and offers a refreshing slice of everyday Sri Lankan life amidst the tourist development, with colourful fish and vegetable markets. A few kilometres inland lies the picture-perfect little estate of **Brief**

Island temple off the coast of Hikkaduwa

Garden (daily 8am–5pm; charge), comprising a small but exquisite garden surrounding an artfully restored colonial villa stuffed full of artworks, photographs and other intriguing mementos collected by its former owner, Bewis Bawa, a famous Sri Lankan socialite, amateur artist and man-of-letters.

Brief Garden

Bewis's work in transforming Brief Garden inspired his brother, the great architect Geoffrey Bawa, to create a similar estate of his own at nearby **Lunuganga** (tours daily 9am–5pm; charge). Over four decades Bawa systematically enlarged and transformed the original house while adding a sculpture gallery, a string of quaint new outbuildings and sylvan terraced gardens overlooking the adjacent lagoon.

About 10km (6 miles) south of Lunuganga, **Kosgoda** beach is a favourite nesting site for marine turtles, with local villagers leading nightly turtle watches. Another 8km (5 miles) south, the village of **Balapitiya** is the starting point for rewarding boat trips along the Madu Ganga, dotted with over fifty islands and rich in local bird life.

Ambalangoda

About 25km (15 miles) south of Bentota, the small town of **Ambalangoda** is best known as the centre of the Sri Lankan mask-making industry, whose grotesque faces, representing various demons and humans, leer at you from shops and houses all over the south of the island. A copious selection of masks, and descriptions of the dances they were originally designed for, can be seen in the **Ariyapala and Sons Mask**

Mask ritual

Sri Lanka's most popular mask is Gurulu Raksha, a terrifying bird-like creature who is believed to prey on snakes and demons. Many people in the south hang Gurulu Raksha masks outside their houses to ward off malign influences.

Museum (daily 8.30am–5.30pm; donation requested). If you want to see the masks used in the dances for which they were originally intended, you may be able to watch rehearsals by students at the nearby Bandu Wijesurya School of Dance.

Some 6km (4 miles) inland from Ambalangoda, the obscure village of **Karandeniya** is home to Sri Lanka's longest reclining Buddha – a super-sized collosus, the best part of 40m (130ft) long.

Hikkaduwa

Close to the southernmost point of the west coast, **Hikkaduwa** offers a down-at-heel alternative to the big resorts further north. Back in the 1970s, Hikkaduwa was Sri Lanka's original hippy hangout, and although uncontrolled development here has taken a massive toll on the beach and town, the resort remains modestly popular amongst backpackers, surfers and divers, and has a liveliness lacking in the sedate resorts further up the coast – while the launch of the hugely successful Hikkaduwa Beach Festival in 2008 gave the town a much needed shot in the arm. The famous **Coral Sanctuary**, a once-beautiful section of reef in shallow water just off the beach in the centre of town, is worth a visit. Hikkaduwa also offers some of the best surfing in Sri Lanka, as well as the island's largest selection of diving schools.

THE SOUTH

In many ways, the south is Sri Lanka at its most quintessentially Sri Lankan, with thousands of comatose villages, nestled under great swathes of palm trees, where the pace of life still travels at the speed of the bicycle rather than the car, and where coconuts are considered more important than computers. For visitors, the region offers a beguiling mixture of culture and hedonism. A long sequence of beautiful and largely unspoilt beaches is interspersed with national parks and some important Buddhist shrines – physical evidence of the south's traditional role as a bastion of Sinhalese Buddhist culture.

Galle

The gateway to the south is the beautiful old settlement of **Galle** (pronounced 'Gaul'), Sri Lanka's best-preserved colonial city. First established by the Portuguese, the old part of the city, known as **Galle Fort**, achieved its present shape largely thanks to the Dutch, who erected a great chain of walls and bastions to protect the settlement from invaders. The streets inside are filled with atmospheric villas hidden behind enormous, shady verandahs and topped with crumbling red-tiled roofs – a wonderful place for an aimless and pleasantly traffic-free stroll.

Palm-fringed coast at Galle

Galle's Historical Mansion Museum

Entrance to the town is through the **Main Gate**, a narrow portal cut into the enormous bastions, facing the cricket ground and modern city. From here, Church Street veers round to the left, taking you past several of Galle's main sights, including the rather dull **Galle National Museum** (Tue–Sat 9am–5pm; charge) and the ultra-deluxe colonial **Amangalla hotel**, occupying a building originally constructed for the Dutch governor in 1684. Just past here is the intriguing **Dutch Reformed Church** of 1755: elegantly Italianate on the outside; severely plain within, apart from the many elaborately carved memorials to the city's Dutch and British settlers.

Continue south to the junction with Queen's Street, marked by a further clutch of colonial buildings, including **All Saint's Church**, whose chunky little spire provides an important city landmark, and the sprawling orange bulk of the **Great Warehouse**. The latter now provides a home for the new **National Maritime Museum** (Tue–Sat 9am–5pm; charge), with a mildly interesting collection of old naval artefacts). Heading south along Leyn Baan Street brings you to the quirky **Historical Mansion Museum** (daily 9am–6pm; donation requested), home to a vast collection of antiques and bric-a-brac assembled by its owner over the past 35 years. At the southern end of Leyn Baan Street is the florid **Meeran Jumma Mosque** and the **lighthouse**, from where it is possible to walk (clockwise) around the bastions all the way back to the Main Gate.

Unawatuna to Mirissa

Past Galle, the coast is dotted with a string of small villages, which survive on a mixture of fishing, coconut farming and low-level tourism. A few kilometres beyond Galle lies the personable little village of **Unawatuna**, which has long-since ◄ ❾ taken over from Hikkaduwa as Sri Lanka's most popular backpacker destination. A beautiful semi-circular beach is backed by a cluster of informal little guesthouses whose rickety wooden structures and string of beachfront cafés lend the place a genuine ad hoc charm. Past Unawatuna, the coastal highway runs close to the sea, running through the small town of **Koggala**, home to the interesting **Martin Wickramasinghe Museum** (daily 9am–5pm; charge), with an intriguing collection of local artefacts relating to the traditional Sinhalese way of life. Beyond Koggala, the town of **Ahangama** is one of the best places in Sri Lanka to see the famous

Stilt fisherman of Ahangama

Rocky myth

The enormous rocky outcrop backing Unawatuna village, Rumassala, is popularly believed to have been dropped by the monkey god Hanuman during his adventures in Sri Lanka described in the great Indian epic, the *Ramayana*.

stilt fishermen, who sit perched on poles amidst the waves casting their lines in the waters. Immediately beyond Ahangama, the village of **Midigama** has a narrow beach, a handful of simple guesthouses and some of Sri Lanka's best surf.

The next town of any consequence along the coastal highway is **Weligama**, a sleepy little place whose quiet streets are lined with chintzy villas decorated with ornately carved wooden eaves. In front of the town, the wide sweep of Weligama Bay is dotted with a couple of tiny islets, most notably **Taprobane**, topped by a crown of tropical greenery. The beach here is long, wide and largely untouched, although most visitors now prefer to crash out at the tiny village of **Mirissa**, on the headland at the far end of the bay, where a small stretch of golden sand nestles beautifully behind a thick screen of palm trees. Mirissa is also the centre for Sri Lanka's burgeoning whale-watching scene; trips can be arranged through Mirissa Water Sports (www.mirissawatersports.com) in the village.

Matara

A few kilometres beyond Mirissa, the bustling little city of **Matara** is the only settlement of any significant size in the south besides Galle. Like Galle, Matara rose to prominence under the Dutch, who fortified the town and made it an important settlement in the elephant and cinnamon trade. A line of coral-stone ramparts divides the modern city from the old colonial district, or **Fort**, which is bisected by peaceful streets of decaying old villas.

Much of the modern town lies on the north side of the palm-lined waters of the Nilwala Ganga river, and it is worth crossing over to visit the quaint little Dutch **Star Fort** of 1763, now home to a modest museum. A couple of kilometres outside town, the modern temple at **Weherehena** is home to one of the biggest Buddhas in the island, a 39m (129ft) gaudily painted colossus seated in deep meditation.

Tangalla and Around

There is another decent beach (and some good snorkelling) in the suburbs of Matara at **Polhena**, but most foreign tourists press on either west to Mirissa and Unawatuna, or further east to **Tangalla**, where more beaches dot the coast on either side of the scruffy little town. Although the beaches here are not as nice as others along the south coast, Tangalla has the bonus of a number of interesting sights in the

Fishing boats at Weligama

surrounding countryside, which are easily combined in a half-day's excursion. These include the unusual blowhole at **Hoo-amaniya**, where a narrow cleft in the rock at the edge of the ocean sends enormous plumes of water up to 15m (50ft) high into the air; and the temple at **Wewurukannala**, whose impressive complex is home to another gigantic Buddha statue; at around 50m (160ft) high even bigger than the one at Weherehena.

Close to Tangalla is another major man-made attraction: the rock temples of **Mulkirigala** (daily 6am–6pm; charge). Something of a cross between Dambulla and Sigiriya, the temples are carved into the flanks of a majestic rocky outcrop which rises dramatically out of the predominantly flat surrounding landscape. Seven hundred steps lead to the top, passing a sequence of temples arranged on four terraces and filled with ornate Buddha statues and wall paintings dating back to the 18th century. At the top, the effort of the climb is rewarded by marvellous views south to the coast and north to the rolling uplands of the hill country.

The temple at Wewurukannala

Bundala National Park

Continuing east along the coast from Tangalla brings you to **Rekawa**, whose beach is one of the most important turtle-nesting sites in the islands. Locals here organise ad hoc nightly turtle watches (charge), during which it is possible to get a glimpse of these majestic creatures dragging themselves laboriously up onto the beach to bury their eggs in the sand.

Beyond Rekawa, the landscape changes as you enter the island's dry zone, the lush palm forests of the west and southwest coasts giving way to an arid, savannah-like scenery which receives far less rainfall than the areas behind. The first of the area's two excellent national parks, **Bundala National Park** (daily 6.30am–6.30pm; charge), is famous principally for the immensely varied aquatic and other bird life found in the park's coastal wetlands and lagoons. Almost 200 species of bird have been recorded here, including the prolific flocks of greater flamingos which arrive from northern India. A large population of wild peacocks adds a distinctive and colourful flourish to the park's tangled grey-green woodlands. Birds apart, Bundala is also home to a rich stock of wildlife including troupes of hyperactive grey langur monkeys, a small number of elephants and ferocious-looking crocodiles, plus sloth bears, civets, giant squirrels and the occasional leopard.

Tissamaharama and Yala

Beyond Bundala the coastal highway veers inland to reach the pleasant town of **Tissamaharama** (usually shortened to 'Tissa'). The town offers a convenient base for trips to Bundala and Yala National Parks, as well as the temple town of

---

Turtle talk

Turtles are amongst the oldest reptiles on the planet, offering a living link with the age of the dinosaurs. They can grow to up to 3m (10ft) in length, live more than 100 years, dive to depths of a kilometre and hold their breath for half an hour – as well as migrating for distances of up to 5,000km (3,000 miles).

An inquisitive giant squirrel

Kataragama, but is also of some historical interest in its own right, occupying the site of the ancient former southern capital of Mahagama. A trio of large stupas strung across the town attest to its former importance, as does the beautiful **Tissa Wewa**, an artificial lake just north of the modern town centre created in the 2nd or 3rd century BC.

For most visitors, Tissamaharama's major attraction is its proximity to **Yala** **National Park** (daily 6.30am–6.30pm; charge), one of the largest and certainly the most popular in Sri Lanka. The principal attraction here is leopards (Yala has one of the densest concentrations of these elusive felines anywhere in the world), while there are also elephants, sloth bears, spotted deer, mongooses, porcupines and a compelling array of bird life.

Kataragama

Inland from Tissa lies the remote temple town of **Kataragama**, one of the island's most revered pilgrimage sites, held sacred by Buddhists, Hindus and Muslims alike. The town owes its importance to the presence here of the island's principal shrine to the god Kataragama, a deity of typically confused Sri Lankan lineage.

Named after the town in which his shrine is located, Kataragama is seen by Sinhalese Buddhists as one of the island's four great protective deities. Sri Lankan Tamils regard him as a local manifestation of the great Hindu god

Skanda, son of Shiva, lending the shrine a multi-faith significance which transcends strict ethnic and religious divides.

Kataragama's shrine, and that of other attendant deities, plus a large stupa and a mosque, occupy the so-called **Sacred Precinct**, a pleasant area of parkland populated by innumerable curious grey langur monkeys and separated from the modern town by the Menik Ganga, in whose waters pilgrims bathe before approaching the temple. The town and temple are quiet by day, but come dramatically alive during the nightly puja, with musicians, singers, dancers and crowds of pilgrims bowed down with huge bowls of fruit as offerings. The scene is at its most dramatic during the annual **Kataragama Festival** (July/Aug), when the god's more ecstatic followers perform gruesome acts of devotion and penance including walking across burning coals and piercing their flesh with long metal skewers.

Drummers at Kataragama

KANDY

Nestled amongst spectacular green mountains at the heart of the hill country, **Kandy** is the definitive Sri Lankan city, home to the country's most revered shrine, its most vibrant performing arts tradition and its greatest festival, the Esala Perahera *(see page 99)*. The last bastion of independent Sinhalese rule in Sri Lanka, the Kandyan Kingdom served as the crucible of the island's distinctive Sinhalese Buddhist culture, resisting repeated attacks by the Portuguese and Dutch before finally falling to the British in 1815.

Kandy is now the island's second-largest city, but although there are crowds and traffic aplenty, the city's low-rise streets, numerous historic monuments and extensive tracts of surrounding greenery lend it a refreshing small-town atmosphere compared with the great sprawl of Colombo. There is

Kandy's lakeside Temple of the Tooth

enough in the town and surrounding countryside to keep anyone occupied for weeks, ranging from Buddhist temples to elephant sanctuaries, and a visit of at least a day or two is an essential part of any tour of the island.

The Lake and Around

Traditional Kandyan dancer

The centre is dominated by the large artificial **Kandy Lake**, created by the last king of Kandy, the infamous Sri Wickrama Rajasinha, using forced labour, although its placid waters give no hint of its unsavoury origins. Just south of the lake, the small **Royal Palace Park** offers fine views over the town and temples. There are even more extensive views from Rajapihilla Mawatha, a road that winds high above the southern side of the lake, giving incomparable panoramas across the city. The city centre, to the west of the lake, consists of a tight grid of busy streets overlooked by the vast **Bahiravakanda Buddha**, posed serenely on a hill overhead.

The dense green forest covering the steep hillside immediately behind the Temple of the Tooth is part of the beautiful **Udawattakele Sanctuary** (daily 6am–6pm; charge), a totally unexpected miniature, tropical wilderness almost in the heart of the centre of town. There are paths and tracks through the woods which are home to a rich array of bird life, the occasional monkey and (if it has been raining) a considerable number of leeches. It's a beautiful spot, though a hefty entrance charge is levied on foreign visitors.

Temple of the Tooth

C ▶ The **Temple of the Tooth**, or Dalada Maligawa (daily 6am–8pm; charge), is home to Sri Lanka's most revered religious relic, the **Buddha's Tooth**, which attracts pilgrims from across the island, and indeed from many other Buddhist countries around Asia. Sitting on the north shore of the lake, the temple comprises a picturesque complex of neat white buildings topped with hipped roofs, framed against the luxuriant green slopes of the Udawattakele Sanctuary, and the entire ensemble is beautifully reflected in the waters of the lake.

Heavy security marks the approach to the temple, the result of an LTTE bomb attack in 1998 which badly damaged the facade. Beyond the various checkpoints, an elegant white outer wall and moat enclose the temple, while to the left is an eye-catching octagonal tower, the **Pittirippuva**, from

The Buddha's Tooth

One of the world's most revered Buddhist relics, the Buddha's Tooth was recovered from the master's funeral pyre at Kushinagar in north India in 543BC and, following the decline in Buddhism in India, smuggled into Sri Lanka in the 4th century AD. Once in Sri Lanka, the Tooth Relic developed into the defining symbol of Sinhalese sovereignty, so that whoever possessed it was believed to hold the right to rule the island, lending it a unique political as well as a spiritual importance. The Tooth Relic was first taken to Anuradhapura, then to Polonnaruwa, and then to various other places around the island before finally arriving in Kandy in 1592, where it became the focus of the massive Esala Perahera festival (see page 99). Security concerns mean that the Tooth Relic is now only rarely put on display to the general public, though its appeal amongst Sri Lankan Buddhists remains undimmed. Its exact nature remains unclear, however – one sceptical Portuguese visitor suggested that its unusual size was due to the fact that it originally belonged to a buffalo.

which all new Sri Lankan heads of state come to address the nation.

Inside, the temple buildings cluster around a single, surprisingly small courtyard, in the middle of which stands the **Tooth Relic shrine**, ornately decorated with wall paintings, elephant tusks, richly carved stone pillars and three lavishly carved doors. The tooth itself is

Inside the Tooth Relic Shrine

housed in a room on the upper storey of the shrine, which is opened for daily pujas at 6am, 9am and 6.30pm, a ceremony enlivened with exuberant Kandyan drumming. The tooth remains locked carefully away in an elaborate golden reliquary in the innermost room of the shrine, and is shown only to the most important of visitors. At the rear of the courtyard, the modern **Alut Maligawa** shrine, built in 1956, houses a large collection of Buddha statues donated by Buddhists from all over the world. The rooms above this are home to the **Sri Dalada Museum** which is devoted to the Tooth Relic, and in particular to the large and eclectic selection of gifts presented as offerings to it over the centuries.

Royal Palace Complex

The Temple of the Tooth was formerly just one part of the **Royal Palace** complex, home to the kings of Kandy, whose surviving buildings enclose the temple and now house a sequence of museums. Exiting the temple to the north brings you to the imposing **Audience Hall**, a grand pavilion whose characteristic hipped roof is supported by dozens of lavishly carved wooden pillars – a classic example of open-plan

Kandyan dancing

Performances of Kandyan dancing and drumming are staged nightly at several venues around town – touristy but enjoyable spectacles in which sumptuously costumed dancers perform superbly acrobatic routines to an accompaniment of wildly energetic drum beats.

Kandyan-style architecture. Just beyond here, a more modest building houses the **Raja Tusker Museum**, home to the stuffed remains of the much-loved Raja, a magnificent pachyderm which was until his death in 1988 the leading elephant in the city's Esala Perahera festival.

To reach the remaining buildings of the Royal Palace, it is necessary to leave the temple and head outside along the shore of the lake. On the lakefront by the south side of the temple lies another striking Kandyan-style building, the two-storey **Royal Bathouse** (Ulpenge). Immediately beyond is the extensive **National Museum** (Tue–Sat 9am–5.30pm; charge), which houses an extensive collection of antique Kandyan artefacts ranging from palm-leaf manuscripts to ivory jewellery. Continue away from the lake past the British courts to reach the **Archaeological Museum** (Wed–Mon; admission with Cultural Triangle ticket – see page 63 – or by donation). Housed in a fine old building which was formerly the king's palace, it is now home to a jumble of old stone carvings, pillars and pots. Finally, hidden behind the National Museum, the lovingly restored **Kandy Garrison Cemetery** is home to an atmospheric cluster of memorials to the city's early British inhabitants, the inscriptions on the headstones painting a vivid picture of the perils of life in the tropics in the 19th century.

The Devales

The northern side of the Temple of the Tooth precinct is bounded by the atmospheric enclosures of the three devales (temples), dedicated to three of the four deities who are traditionally thought to protect the Kandyan kingdom (the fourth devale, an interesting little shrine dedicated to the god Kataragama, lies nearby in the city centre on Kotugodelle Vidiya). Approached through a gateway to the left of the entrance to the Temple of the Tooth, the **Pattini Devale** is dominated by an enormous bo tree raised on a huge stone platform. The temple itself, a small but lavishly decorated building, stands just to the right of the entrance. Next to here is the Victorian **St Paul's Church**, an incongruous Anglican intrusion in this most sacred Buddhist precinct, whose beautifully preserved interior offers a moving memorial to the city's early British settlers.

Continue through the Pattini Devale to reach the **Natha Devale**, a quaint collection of stupas and small shrines. Its principal shrine (on the south side of the enclosure), occupies a diminutive stone building, topped by an Indian-style *shikhara* dome, which is the oldest building in Kandy. Heading left out of the Natha Devale brings you to the finest of the three devales, the **Vishnu Devale**, whose main building, approached via a long flight of steps, houses a wooden pavilion, or *digge*, traditionally used as a practice venue by the city's drummers and dancers.

Botanical Garden blooms

Peradeniya Botanical Gardens

The countryside around Kandy offers several rewarding day trips. Just 6km (4 miles) outside the city, the extensive **Peradeniya Botanical Gardens** (daily 7.30am–5.45pm; charge) are the finest in the country, home to a vast array of tropical flora set in a bend in the Mahaweli Ganga. The minimal signage means that non-botanists will struggle to get a full sense of what they are seeing, although the basic map available at the entrance gives a rough idea of the gardens' layout and content. From the entrance, the stately, much-photographed **Royal Palm Avenue** leads down to the Great Lawn at the centre of the gardens, where a massive Javan fig has created an enormous arboreal pavilion, normally busy with picnicking locals. Beyond here, the northern section of the gardens is the wildest, home to an enormous population of fruit bats who hang in great clusters from the trees overhead.

Pinnewala Elephant Orphanage

An hour's drive west of Kandy lies one of the island's most popular attractions, the outstanding **Pinnewala Elephant Orphanage** (daily 8.30am–6pm; charge), the world's largest collection of captive elephants. The orphanage is home to more than 80 animals orphaned or injured in the wild, mainly as a result of the innumerable clashes between elephants and villagers which, sadly, are an ongoing feature of life in the island – as well as an increasing number of elephants born here in captivity. The elephants range in age from the stately elderly matriarchs to the tiniest and cutest of baby pachyderms.

Injured elephants

Pinnewala's elephants include one blind elephant, Raja, and one with only three legs, christened Sama, who had the misfortune to step on a landmine laid during the civil war.

Residents of the Elephant Orphanage

Visits are best timed to coincide with the three daily feeding and bathing sessions (9.15am, 1.15pm and 5pm). During the feeding sessions, the younger elephants are hand-fed from enormous bottles of milk, while twice daily the entire herd is driven down to the Ma Oya river to splash around in the water for an hour or so – a marvellous sight not to be missed, despite the fact that the elephants are regularly outnumbered by the hordes of camera-toting tourists who congregate for the spectacle.

The only drawback to Pinnewala is that it is not possible to interact with the elephants, or to learn much about them. For this, you'll need to visit the nearby **Millennium Elephant Foundation** (daily 8am–5pm; charge), home to nine elephants (mostly retured working animals) and a good place to learn more about their role in Sri Lankan life and culture; they also run elephant-related volunteer programmes to help the animals.

THE HILL COUNTRY

Occupying the southern heart of the island, the hill country is Sri Lanka at its most scenic: a magnificent region of precipitous green mountains carpeted with lush tea plantations and dotted with tumbling waterfalls and old-world British colonial memorabilia – gothic churches, half-timbered villas and rattling railways – which add a quaintly whimsical touch to the highlands' compelling natural attractions.

For most of the country's history this beautiful but rugged region was sparsely populated and, with the exception of the area around Kandy, of minimal political significance. But with the arrival of the British and the introduction of large-scale tea cultivation in the 19th century, the area assumed an increasing economic importance, one that it maintains to this day. The arrival of thousands of Indian Tamils (the so-called

Mountain scenery around Nuwara Eliya

'Plantation Tamils') to work the tea estates added a further splash of ethnic colour to this fascinating region.

Nuwara Eliya and Around

At the heart of the southern hill country lies the old colonial resort of **Nuwara Eliya**, the highest town in Sri Lanka, ◀ 22 dominated by the densely forested bulk of **Pidurutalagala**, or Mount Pedro, the island's tallest peak at 2,524m (8,281ft) (although sadly the summit itself is off limits).

First established by the British in the 19th century, Nuwara Eliya is often touted as Sri Lanka's 'Little England', and although much of the modern town is now an unattractive mess of concrete buildings and noxious traffic fumes, the open spaces of Victoria Park and the golf course add some welcome greenery to the modern centre. The edges of town still sport a fair sprinkling of atmospheric colonial-era villas and hotels whose incongruous architecture – a mix of fake-half timbering and brightly painted seaside-style architecture – add a pleasant touch of old-world charm. Many of the town's colonial-era buildings have now been converted into engagingly atmospheric hotels, most strikingly Jetwing St Andrew's, the Grand and, most famously, the Hill Club, a venerable old stone building whose nostalgic interior offers a memorable glimpse of colonial life in the tropics.

The town also makes an excellent base for exploring the surrounding region, and has wonderful scenery in its immediate vicinity, most easily enjoyed by making the short walk up **Single Tree Mountain**, from where there are marvellous panoramas over the surrounding mountains. Slightly further afield are the **Hakgala Botanical Gardens** (daily 8am–5pm; charge), set at the foot of the imposing Hakgala Rock. Established in 1861 as a place to grow cinchona, a source of the anti-malarial drug quinine, the gardens were later planted with an extensive range of local and foreign flora and offer a beautiful retreat from the hustle and bustle of Nuwara Eliya, as well as an excellent place to spot some of Sri Lanka's rare endemic montane bird species.

Nuwara Eliya also lies at the heart of the Sri Lankan tea industry, with mile upon mile of the surrounding hills carpeted in endless swathes of lush green tea bushes. Two local tea plantations welcome visitors: the **Pedro Tea Estate**, just 3km (2 miles) east of town, and the beautiful **Labookelie Estate** further away to the north. Both offer interesting factory tours and see how the leaf is processed, and the chance to wander amongst the immaculately manicured surrounding plantations.

Sri Lankan Tea

The tea industry played a formative role in Sri Lanka's early commercial history, and although it has now been overtaken in importance by the garment-manufacturing and tourist industries, it retains a crucial role in the island's modern economy. Sri Lanka remains the world's second largest exporter of the beverage, after India, and the tea industry accounts for around a quarter of the country's export earnings. The suitability of the island's central highlands – with their wet, elevated and steeply shelving terrain – for tea growing was first recognised by the British, who began enthusiastically establishing plantations here following the collapse of the island's coffee industry in the second half of the 19th-century. Many of the factories and estates they established remain in operation to this day, still largely worked by the descendants of the original 'Plantation Tamils' who were brought by the British from India to address the labour shortage in the highlands. In general, the higher the plantation, the more delicate and sought-after the tea. The so-called 'high-grown' tea from the premier estates around Nuwara Eliya remains amongst the most highly prized in the world market today.

Horton Plains and World's End

The most memorable attraction within striking distance of Nuwara Eliya is **Horton Plains National Park** (daily 6.30am–6.30pm; charge), lying on the very edge of the hill country. The plains are a world away from the humid lowlands: a bleak, mist-shrouded expanse of moorland, more reminiscent of

Harvesting tea

Scotland than a tropical island, dotted with strands of tangled cloud forest. At the southern edge of the park, the unforgettable viewpoint at **World's End** offers perhaps Sri Lanka's finest and most famous panorama (the unpredictable weather permitting; get there early), perched on the edge of a huge, sheer cliff face which plunges almost 1,000m (3,300ft) to the lowland plains below.

Haputale

East of Horton Plains, a string of small towns and villages sit atop the escarpment at the southern edge of the hill country, all offering magnificent views and scenery, extensive tea plantations, and occasional colonial memorabilia.

There are more stunning views from the ramshackle little town of **Haputale**, perched on the very edge of the hills, and memorable walks in the vicinity. The finest route heads out of town to the picturesque **Dambatenne Tea Factory** and its beautiful tea gardens, then climbs up to **Lipton's Seat**, named after the famous Victorian tea magnate whose name still adorns tea bags worldwide, and which is a serious rival to the better known World's End viewpoint.

Ella and Around

Monks at Ella Falls

Most visitors, however, press on to **Ella**: a charming little English-style village poised above **Ella Gap**, and offering further superlative views through a narrow cleft in the hills down to the plains below. The village itself is one of the most relaxing places in Sri Lanka to unwind for a few days, with a plethora of small, unassuming but enjoyable guesthouses serving up some of the best home cooking on the island. You can work up an appetite by tackling some of the wonderful walks through the surrounding tea plantations, most notably the short but rewarding hike up **Little Adam's Peak** and the longer, more challenging ascent of **Ella Rock**.

Ella is also a good base from which to explore the area's myriad attractions. Just below the village, the majestic **Rawana Ella Falls** tumble down a series of sheer cliff faces. This is one of the finest of the hill country's many waterfalls and one of several places around Ella named after Rawana, the demonic villain of the great Indian epic the *Ramayana*, who it is claimed imprisoned Rama's wife Sita in a cave nearby. After the Falls, the road hairpins dramatically down to the dog-eared little town of **Wellawaya**, which lies at the foot of the escarpment. Just beyond are the statues of **Buduruwagala**, a majestic sequence of seven figures carved in low relief into a towering rock face and showing, for Sri Lanka, an unusual selection of deities, including the Mahayana Buddhist deities Avalokitesvara and Maitreya alongside the Buddha himself.

Adam's Peak

At the opposite end of the southern hill country, west of Horton's Plains, the soaring summit of **Adam's Peak** towers high over the lowlands below. The mountain is both one of Sri Lanka's most dramatic natural features and also one of its most revered pilgrimage sites thanks to the small and curiously shaped depression on the summit that is popularly claimed to be the Buddha's Footprint, or **Sri Pada**. Not to be left out, the island's Hindus, Muslims and Christians subsequently came up with their own legends claiming that the footprint is that of Shiva, Adam and St Thomas respectively – though none of these claims has ever gathered much popular support.

During the pilgrimage season (Dec/Jan–May), thousands of pilgrims make the arduous ascent up the 4,800 steps that lead to the summit. Traditionally, the climb is made in the

Adam's Peak, the perfect shadow, seen at dawn

cool of the night in order to reach the summit by dawn. In season, the steps are illuminated and dotted with impromptu teashops offering refreshment to weary pilgrims. Not only does this night-time ascent offer the best odds of a cloud-free view from the top, but it also gives you the chance to see the peak's famous shadow, a perfectly triangular mirage cast by the summit, which seems to hang mysteriously in mid-air for 20 minutes or so following sunrise, weather permitting. Buddhists believe that this shadow is a physical representation of the 'Triple Gem', a kind of Buddhist Holy Trinity symbolising the Buddha, his teachings, and the Sangha (a community of Buddhist monks).

Ratnapura and Around

The town of Ratnapura lies directly south of Adam's Peak, though to reach it by road involves a long and circuitous road journey either south through Balangoda or northwest through the dramatic ranges at the western edge of the hill country to **Kitulgala**. Kitulgala is famous as the spectacular location for the filming of the Oscar-winning *The Bridge on the River Kwai* and is now a popular centre for white-water rafting on the choppy waters of the Kelani Ganga.

27 ▶ The sizeable town of **Ratnapura** itself is the largest in the region, pleasantly situated amidst the southern ranges of the hill country and famous as the centre of the island's gem-mining industry. Enormous quantities of precious stones are excavated by hand from the alluvial deposits washed down from the hills here using primitive and labour-intensive mining techniques. You can watch uncut gems being traded in town along **Saviya Street** (though rip-offs are common, and it is best not to buy unless you are an expert gemologist), and it is also possible to arrange visits to local 'mines' (effectively just large holes in the ground) in order to watch local gem-diggers in action.

Uda Walawe and Sinharaja

For many visitors, however, the main attraction of Ratnapura is as a base from which to visit the two outstanding national parks nearby. The popular **Uda Walawe National Park** (daily 6.30am–6.30pm; charge), is just south of the hill country. Although the park's arid and denuded landscape is relatively unimpressive, the lack of forest cover makes it one of the easiest places in the island to spot wildlife, including the park's large elephant population.

West of Uda Walawe, draped over the undulating southern outliers of the hill country, **Sinharaja Forest Reserve** (daily 8am–6pm; charge) protects the island's largest surviving stretch of tropical rainforest. Sinharaja is quite unlike anywhere else on the island. The world inside the forest is positively Amazonian: trees, creepers, ferns, lianas and epiphytes, all tangled together in damp exuberance.

The forest is a treasure box of ecological curiosities containing no fewer than 830 species of endemic flora and fauna, including monkeys, reptiles, many rare bird species and a baffling array of insect life, although the density of the reserve's vegetation and the height of the forest canopy makes wildlife-spotting surprisingly difficult without the services of a trained guide.

Sinharaja rainforest

THE CULTURAL TRIANGLE

Dambulla Rock Cave Temples

North of the hill country stretch the plains of the northern dry zone, a great stretch of hot, denuded savannah, covered in thorny scrub and dotted with dramatic rocky outcrops. Despite the harshness of the natural environment, these plains were home to the remarkable civilisation of the ancient Sinhalese, which flourished here from around the 4th century BC until the 13th century AD. Their cultural, agricultural and architectural achievements ranked amongst the finest in the ancient world, until they were finally destroyed by repeated Tamil invasions.

Following the abandonment of the plains, the region's two great cities and innumerable smaller religious sites were largely abandoned to the jungle until they were recovered by 20th-century archaeologists. Their collective remains – a remarkable array of stupas, temples, palaces, monasteries and monolithic Buddha statues – offer a fascinating insight into the unique arts and culture of Sri Lanka's early Sinhalese people.

This area of the island is now commonly described as the **Cultural Triangle** (with the three points of the imaginary triangle being placed at the cities of Kandy, Anuradhapura and Polonnaruwa). This is a convenient modern tourist name for the region, although it is also, and more accurately, known by its ancient name of **Rajarata**, or 'The King's Land'.

North from Kandy to Dambulla

A handful of interesting sights dot the countryside between Kandy and Dambulla, including a trio of temples which merit a visit on the journey north. The first, right next to the main highway, just north of the town of Matale is **Aluvihara**, an interesting Buddhist monastic complex featuring a sequence of cave temples hidden amidst enormous rock outcrops.

The complex is famous mainly for being the place where the principal Buddhist scriptures, the *Tripitakaya*, were first written down, an event which had enormous significance in the international development of the religion.

Hidden away a few miles west of the highway in a beautiful rural location in the village of Ridigama, **Ridi Vihara** is one of the most interesting small temples on the island, housing a range of ancient sculptures and other rare artefacts. Back on the main road and continuing north, the exquisite little stone temple at **Nalanda** (charge, or free with CT ticket), was built as a Buddhist shrine, though in a style which is strongly reminiscent of Hindu Indian architecture, and even includes a couple of erotic carvings, but now heavily eroded almost beyond recognition.

The Cultural Triangle Ticket

The Cultural Triangle (CT) Ticket covers most of the main Cultural Triangle sites, including Anuradhapura, Polonnaruwa and Sigiriya (but not Dambulla). The ticket is available from the main sites or from the CT offices in Kandy and Colombo; it costs $50 and is valid for one entry to each site for 14 days from first use. Buying a CT ticket makes good sense if you're visiting more than a couple of the area's principal attractions, since tickets for admission to individual sites can otherwise cost as much as $25.

Dambulla

North of Nalanda, more or less at the centre of the Cultural Triangle, the imposing 160m (52ft) **Dambulla Rock**, just south of the dusty and workaday town of Dambulla, houses the most impressive and venerated Buddhist cave temples. There are five temples here, filled with a veritable treasury of Buddhist art, including innumerable statues of the Buddha and other deities, plus the finest selection of murals on the island.

The finest of the rock temples, Caves 2 and 3, are masterpieces of Sinhalese art. Cave 3, the **Maha Alut Viharaya**, reaches a height of 10m (33ft), with a sloping roof which gives it the appearance of an enormous tent. As well as the cave's fine Buddha statues, some carved from solid rock, there are outstanding murals (look up at the ceiling as you enter the cave) showing the Buddha preaching and (to the left of the entrance) a statue of the Kandyan king Kirti Sri Rajasinha, who was largely responsible for the temples' 18th-century embellishments.

Even larger and finer is Cave 2, the **Maharaja Vihara**, a vast underground space some 50m (165ft) long crammed full of religious artworks, including more than a hundred Buddhas ranged around the walls in various poses. There is also an eye-boggling collection of mu-

Maharajah Vihara at Dambulla

rals, including the extraordinary **Mara Parajaya**, showing the Buddha's defeat of Mara and his massed regiments of hairy demons; and the seductive **Daughters of Mara**, in which the Buddha is shown resisting the considerable attractions of the demon's legion of comely daughters.

Sigiriya

Sri Lanka's most remarkable single attraction, the spectacular citadel of **Sigiriya** (daily 7am–6pm; admission with CT ticket), sits atop a vast gneiss outcrop which towers more than 200m (650ft) above the surrounding plains at the heart of the Cultural Triangle. The citadel was established in the

5th century by the infamous Kassapa, who murdered his father and assumed the kingship of the island, establishing a new and impregnable fortress-palace atop Sigiriya rock. Kassapa ruled the island from here for 18 years before being killed in battle, after which Sigiriya was abandoned.

The entire eastern side of the rock is surrounded by an extensive moat, past which an avenue arrows towards the rock, crossing a series of elaborate pleasure gardens. The first section, the **Water Gardens**, consists of an elaborate arrangement of pools and fountains, beyond which are the much more naturalistic **Boulder Gardens**, littered with massive rocks. Several of the caves found here were also home to reclusive monks, and still bear slight traces of murals, while some of the boulders have been carved into 'thrones' which probably had a symbolic religious significance.

School trip to Sigiriya

Past the Boulder Gardens, steps climb with increasing steepness up to the base of the rock itself. Close to the foot of the rock, a pair of incongruous Victorian metal spiral staircases lead up to the much celebrated **Sigiriya Damsels**, one of Sri Lanka's most famous sights: a little picture gallery showing around 20 beautiful bare-breasted nymphs floating on a sea of clouds. Immediately past the damsels, the pathway up the rock is flanked by the **Mirror Wall**, whose brightly polished surface is inscribed with hundreds of ancient graffiti messages recording early visitors' impressions of the site – and the nearby damsels in particular. Many are of considerable poetic value, and an important source for historians of Sinhalese language and script.

Further steps lead onwards and upwards to the **Lion Platform**, embellished

Sigiriya Damsel

with two enormous stone paws, all that remains of the open-mouthed lion which originally guarded the final ascent to the summit of the rock and Kassapa's palace. Metal steps lead between the paws and up to the summit, clinging to the bare rock face (and presenting something of a challenge to sufferers of vertigo). The summit itself is covered in the slight remains of Kassapa's palace, although the great jumble of brick foundations is difficult to interpret and far less impressive than the stupendous views down over the Water Gardens below and the plains stretching away in every direction.

Polonnaruwa

Another of Sri Lanka's great ruined cities, **Polonnaruwa** was capital of the island for a far shorter period of time. It enjoyed a brief but exuberant cultural flowering during its 150 years of pre-eminence from 1056 to 1215, during which Sinhalese art and architecture reached new heights of artistry. The **ruins** (daily 7am–6pm; charge, or free with CT ticket) here are more

Polonnaruwa

```
0    500 m
0    500 yds
```

compact, more varied and much more easily digestible than those at Anuradhapura, although it is also more of a museum piece and lacks something of Anuradhapura's enduring religious vibrancy.

Before entering the site itself, make time for the excellent **Polonnaruwa Museum** (daily 9am–6pm; admission with CT ticket), the best in the island, with its insightful displays on life in the ancient capital, and some fine exhibits including a number of superb Chola bronzes recovered from the site.

The Citadel

Close to the entrance, the buildings of the **Citadel** (or Royal Palace Group) comprise the substantial remains of the palace built by the city's most famous king, Parakramabahu the Great (reigned 1153–86), who was responsible for many of the city's most impressive structures, though his lust for building and weakness for ill-advised military campaigns almost bankrupted the kingdom. The remains of the **Vejayanta Pasada** (Royal Palace)  itself are large but rather plain. More impressive is the **Council Chamber**, the king's audience hall, whose finely carved base is decorated with dwarfs and galloping elephants and topped with a pair of superb lion statues – the defining symbol of Sinhalese royalty. Just northeast of here, look out for the finely preserved **Kumara Pokuna** (Royal Baths).

The Quadrangle

Contained in a small enclosure just north of the Royal Palace is the remarkable cluster of buildings known as the **Quadrangle**. This was the religious heart of the city, home to the famous Tooth Relic *(see page 48)*, which was housed here in various temples. The finest of these is the magnificent **Vatadage**, probably the most beautiful building in Sri Lanka, a glorious circular structure decorated in a riot of carving,

The Vatadage at Polonnaruwa

Cycle the site

Hiring a bicycle is the most enjoyable way to explore Polonnaruwa. The flat, traffic-free roads through the site make it one of Sri Lanka's most enjoyable two-wheel experiences.

with four sumptuous staircases, each embellished with a moonstone, and a *makara*-decorated balustrade.

Numerous other remains stand cheek-by-jowl around the enclosure. The most obviously impressive is the **Thuparama**, a solid and unusually well preserved structure whose exterior carvings show distinct Hindu influence, the result of the powerful coterie of Tamil mercenaries and other Indians who made the city their home. Other notable buildings include the **Hatadage**, another temple which once housed the Tooth Relic; the uniquely Khmer-style **Sathmahal Pasada**; the beautiful **Lotus Madapa** pavilion; and the enormous **Gal Potha**, a huge rock inscription recording the real and imagined exploits of Nissanka Malla, a famously boastful Polonnaruwan king whose self-glorifying inscriptions can be found all over the city. Immediately south of the Quadrangle is the very Indian-looking **Shiva Devale No. 1**, one of many Hindu temples at the site, built by the Tamil Pandyans who conquered the city in the 13th century.

The Alahana Pirivena and Beyond

D▶ North of the Quadrangle lie the extensive remains of the **Alahana Pirivena**, the city's most important monastery. The first notable sight here is the monumental **Rankot Vihara**, the only stupa at Polonnaruwa to rival the great examples at Anuradhapura. Continuing north, the heart of the monastery is marked by a cluster of exceptional buildings, including the **Lankatilake**, a narrow shrine enclosing a huge – though headless – standing Buddha; the **Kiri Vihara**, a fine, delicately built stupa; and the **Buddha Sima Pasada**, the monastery's chapter house. Finest of all, however, is the **Gal Vihara**, further north, one of the island's most famous shrines, comprising a line of four monumental stone Buddhas including a vast reclining Buddha, the most famous statue in Sri Lanka, and, next to it, a unique standing figure with arms crossed who is sometimes thought to represent Ananda, the Buddha's most devoted follower.

Continuing north, you pass the gargantuan **Demala Maha Seya** stupa, almost buried in vegetation, before reaching the **Tivanka Patamaghara**, another Buddhist shrine built in a heavily Indianised architectural style, exemplified by the finely carved niched windows which decorate its exterior. Inside, a sequence of outstanding (though difficult to see) frescoes of Hindu-style deities in elaborate tiaras cover the walls.

The majestic reclining Buddha

The Southern Remains

Further interesting remains lie south of the main site along the shores of the vast **Parakrama Samudra**, one of the greatest of the enormous artificial lakes, or 'tanks', built for irrigation by the ancient Sinhalese *(see page 76)*. The so-called **Island Gardens** (or Rest House Group), almost in the middle of the little modern town centre, are home to the modest remnants of Nissanka Malla's palace, while further south lies the **Pothgul Vihara**, a circular shrine, and the famous statue of a bearded figure holding a palm-leaf manuscript, either a sage or Parakramabahu himself, depending on who you believe.

Minneriya and Kaudulla

If you have had enough of Buddhist remains, a pair of outstanding national parks lie close to Polonnaruwa. **Minneriya** and **Kaudulla National Parks** (both daily 6.30am–6.30pm; charge) are famous mainly for their extensive elephant populations. The parks form part of an 'elephant corridor', and the animals migrate seasonally between the two reserves, depending on water levels in the local tanks (local guides will be able to tell you which of the two parks offers the best elephant-spotting opportunities at any given time).

Elephant in the National Park

Yapahuwa to Ritigala

On the eastern edge of the Cultural Triangle, the ruined citadel of **Yapahuwa** (daily 8am–6pm; charge) is all that remains of one of the many short-lived Sinhalese capitals which were established and then abandoned in rapid succession during the chaotic 13th and 14th centuries. The royal palace formerly stood atop the enormous rocky outcrop which forms the centrepiece of the site, although the main attraction is the spectacular stone staircase which climbs up the rock with dizzying steepness, and is sumptuously decorated with statues of elephants, dwarfs, goddesses and a pair of pop-eyed stone lions. The remains of a few other buildings and a small museum stand at the foot of the steps.

Abandoned Buddha

A legend states that the Aukana Buddha was carved by a master sculptor and the Sasseruwa Buddha by his apprentice – and that the student, on seeing the excellence of his teacher's creation, abandoned his own statue in despair.

Northeast of Yapahuwa is the **Aukana Buddha**, a 12m **35** (39ft) high statue of a standing Buddha which has become one of Sri Lanka's most famous icons – a mighty and austerely simple figure, best seen at dawn when the low light reveals the stone's fine detail (the name Aukana means 'sun-eating'). Nearby is the equally grand **Sasseruwa Buddha**, another monumental, if slightly less finely carved, standing figure – although for many visitors the relative lack of sculptural finish makes it the more humanised and endearing of the two colossi.

Continuing northeast you come to the atmospheric forest monastery of **Ritigala** (admission with CT ticket), the best **36** known of the various woodland retreats to which the island's more ascetic monks withdrew in centuries past. The forest monastery was discovered only in 1872. Buried amongst beautiful lowland dry-zone forest, the monastery's ruins are deeply atmospheric but little understood, consisting of a succession of interlinked courtyards, walkways and the foundations of structures built in a distinctive 'double-platform' style, with pairs of buildings surrounded by miniature moats and linked by tiny bridges – although their exact function remains obscure.

The Aukana Buddha at Anuradhapura

Anuradhapura

At the northern edge of the Cultural Triangle, the great monastic ruined city of **Anuradhapura** was for some 1,500 years the island's capital and cultural fulcrum. One of the greatest monastic cities the world has ever seen, ancient Anuradhapura supported a population of as many as 10,000 monks, and the ruins of its great religious foundations, monumental stupas and enormous man-made lakes continue to inspire awe amongst visitors and pride amongst the island's latter-day Sinhalese.

Most (but not all) of the main sites in Anuradhapura are contained in the **Sacred Precinct**, to the west of the modern town of Anuradhapura, and are covered by the Cultural Triangle Ticket *(see page 63)*. The best way to see the sights is to hire a bicycle, although you will need a couple of days just to cover the main attractions, and far longer if you want to really get to understand the vast and often bewildering sprawl of monuments and ruins which dot the countryside in and around the city.

The Mahavihara

At the centre of the Sacred Precinct are the remains of the great **Mahavihara monastery**, still one of the island's great pilgrimage centres thanks to the presence here of the **Sri Maha Bodhi** (Sacred Bo Tree; donation), a tree of enormous age which was allegedly grown from a cutting from the tree in India under which the Buddha attained enlightenment. The Sri Maha Bodhi is now the focus of worship in Anuradhapura, and always busy with pilgrims and tourists alike.

North of the Sri Maha Bodhi rises the huge, dirty-white hemisphere of the **Ruwanweliseya**, the third largest – and best preserved – stupa in the city, standing in a square com-

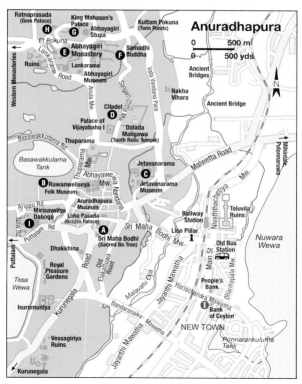

pound whose flanking walls are decorated with dozens of elephant heads. From here a road runs north to another stupa, the **Thuparama**, the oldest in the whole of Sri Lanka and a far more modest structure than the Ruwanweliseya, picturesquely framed by a cluster of lopsided columns which once supported a roof.

The Jetavana Monastery and the Citadel

Another of Anuradhapura's great monasteries, the **Jetavana**, lies just under a kilometre northeast of the Mahavihara. Like the Mahavihara, it is centred around a monumental **stupa**, a colossal brick edifice which once reached a height of 120m (390ft), though it has now been reduced to around 70m (230ft). It remains the world's largest brick-built structure. The area around the stupa is littered with remains, including a fine-

Irrigation in Ancient Sri Lanka

The trio of lakes which surround Anuradhapura are just three of the thousands of man-made reservoirs – or 'tanks' *(wewas)* – that dot Sri Lanka's northern plains. Early Sinhalese civilisation was agricultural, and the lack of regular rainfall in the northern dry zone meant that the storage and distribution of water from the region's few dependable rivers or collected during the brief monsoon, was crucial. The island's first reservoirs and irrigation channels date from the earliest days of Sinhalese settlement, but it was between the 3rd and 7th centuries AD that the vast system of tanks was linked by thousands of miles of irrigation channels in one of the greatest hydraulic achievements the world has seen. Over time, the maintenance of these systems began to place an untenable burden on the population and as waves of Tamil invaders harassed the north, they fell into disarray. Gradually, the water supply failed and the Sinhalese decamped, abandoning the northern plains and moving towards the less arid lands further south.

The impressive Jetavana stupa

ly preserved bathing pool and the unusual 'Buddhist railing', a kind of ancient stone fence. There is also an interesting **museum** (daily 8am–5pm; entrance free with CT ticket) housing an excellent selection of finely crafted items found at the site.

North of the Jetavanarama, the large walled area known as the **Citadel** formerly enclosed the city's royal palace and central commercial district, though little now survives apart from innumerable brick foundations of unidentifiable buildings and the remnants of the **Royal Palace** itself, notable mainly for the pair of fine guard stones at its entrance, showing a pair of unusually fat dwarves.

The Abhayagiri Monastery

Continuing north you come to the **Abhayagiri** monastery, once the largest in Anuradhapura, but now the least visited and therfore most atmospheric area in the city, with a prodigious quantity of foundations, pillars, staircases and eroded

A monk in the shade

brick walls dotted amidst beautiful woodland. Again, a monumental **stupa** lies at the heart of the monastery, still largely unrestored and covered in a thick layer of vegetation. East of the stupa, the famous **Samadhi Buddha** ◀—Ⓕ statue shows the Buddha deep in meditation – a classic Sri Lankan pose, combining simplicity and serenity. Just beyond here are the marvellously well-preserved **Kuttam Pokuna**, two bathing pools which were once used for monks' ritual ablutions.

Further monuments lie scattered in the surrounding woodlands, including **Ma-** ◀—Ⓖ **hasen's Palace**, home to per-

Ⓗ▶ haps the finest moonstone in Sri Lanka; the **Ratnaprasada**, notable for its remarkable guard stone figure; and the gargantuan **Et Pokuna**, or Elephant Pool, the largest bathing pool in the city, and every bit as big as its name suggests. There's also a small **museum** about 500m/yds south of the stupa (daily 8am–5pm; admission with CT ticket) housing a fine collection of statues and other artefacts recovered from the area.

Outlying Remains

Ⓘ▶ A further rewarding clutch of monuments lies south of the Mahavihara, starting with the fine **Mirisavatiya Daboga**, a large white structure confusingly similar in size and appearance to the nearby Ruwanweliseya, which is famous for having been built by King Dutugemunu out of remorse for having thoughtlessly eaten a bowl of chillies without offering any to the city's monks. South of here, the picturesque **Royal Pleasure Gardens** contain two fine bathing pools, one carved with wonderfully naturalistic low-relief elephants. Just beyond is the **Isurumuniya Vihara** (charge; not included in CT ticket), one of the oldest shrines in the city and home to an interesting selection of carvings.

Mihintale

Twelve kilometres (7 miles) east of Anuradhapura, **Mihintale** is revered amongst Sri Lankans as the place at which Buddhism was first introduced to the island. According to legend, it was here that Mahinda, and envoy of the great Indian Buddhist emperor Asoka, converted the Sinhalese king Devanampiya Tissa and his followers in 247BC.

The site is deeply atmospheric, with a sequence of stupas and other remains scattered across a sequence of hilltops linked by beautiful stone stairways and shaded by innumerable frangipani trees.

After the car park, the site **museum** (Wed–Mon) and the ruins of a medieval hospital, stone steps lead up to the remains of the **Medamaluwa monastery**. The remains include two huge stone troughs which would have originally been filled daily by devotees with rice for the monastery's monks, and a pair of ancient stone tablets on which are written the rules of monastic life. From here, a long line of steps leads to the centre of

Steps at Kuttam Pokuna

Mihintale (charge) and the small **Ambasthala Stupa**, allegedly marking the exact spot at which Mahinda converted Devanampiya Tissa. Steps lead from here to a cluster of further remains, including the dramatic **Aradhana Gala** rocky outcrop, from which Mahinda preached his first sermon, and up again to the **Mahaseya Stupa**, from where there are marvellous views out over the surrounding plains to the great stupas of Anuradhapura, clearly visible in the distance.

THE EAST

Sri Lanka's east is one of the poorest and most sparsely populated regions on the island thanks to its arid climate and inhospitable terrain. The area's fortunes were further blighted by the civil war, whose fluctuating front line ran through the region and pitted its inhabitants – a varied mix of Tamils, Sinhalese and Muslims – against one another in recurrent bouts of communal blood-letting, and by the Asian tsunami in 2004, which wreaked havoc all along the coast. For the visitor, the region's major attractions are at present limited to a handful of beaches and the little city of Trincomalee.

Unrequited love

Lover's Leap was named in honour of a young Dutch lady named Francina van Rhede who, according to tradition, jumped off Swami Rock after having been abandoned by her lover – although colonial records suggest that not only did she survive the fall, but that she also subsequently married someone else.

Trincomalee

The principal city of the east, **Trincomalee** (or 'Trinco'), ◀ 39 is Sri Lanka's most ethnically diverse city, its population divided almost equally between Tamils, Sinhalese and Muslims. Repeated clashes between these different ethnic groups made the city the most volatile in the island throughout the civil war, and

Lover's Leap on the Swami Rock

have continued to overshadow its fortunes during the subsequent ceasefire. Although parts of the city are scruffy and unappealing, its magnificent natural setting and faded colonial atmosphere lend it an understated but palpable charm.

Trinco's most interesting area, occupying a narrow promontory dividing Dutch and Back bays, is **Fort Frederick**, the old British fort, surrounded by substantial ramparts enclosing a tranquil stretch of parkland dotted with 19th-century colonial buildings. Entering through the impressive main gate, a road winds up through the fort to **Swami Rock**, a dramatic cliff top rising high at the edge of the promontory above deep-blue waters, with fine views over Back Bay, the town, and the innumerable fishing boats bobbing in the waters below. Perched atop Swami Rock, the **Koneswaram Kovil** is one of the island's holiest Shiva temples, although the building itself is modern and of little interest. Immediately behind the temple, the sheer cliff plunges into the waters at **Lover's Leap**.

East coast beach

Below Swami Rock, the town centre comprises a dusty grid of low-rise streets dotted with colourful little Hindu temples, with pleasant backstreets of decaying colonial villas. At the southeastern end of the centre, the dusty open space of the Esplanade backs the attractive town beach flanking Dutch Bay. Walking across the town centre brings you to **Inner Harbour**, the original source of the city's maritime prosperity and importance and still a grand sight, with large container ships and tanks moored in the distance and lines of hills beyond.

Uppuveli and Nilaveli

Most visitors come to the Trincomalee area to visit the twin resorts of **Uppuveli** and **Nilaveli**, lying on a swathe of beautiful golden sand a few kilometres north of the city. Despite repeated upheavals during the civil war and, more recently, significant tsunami damage, both resorts have somehow kept going against the odds, embodying the sense of enduring optimism which characterises life in the war-torn east and north. Development is at present confined to a couple of large resort hotels and a cluster of low-key guesthouses, and the atmosphere is thoroughly somnolent. Uppuveli is also the jumping-off point for boat and snorkelling trips to nearby **Pigeon Island**, which boasts colourful tropical fish and patches of live coral.

Arugam Bay and Around

The east's most popular tourist destination, the village of **Arugam Bay** is best known for its superb surf. The waves here are the finest on the island, attracting a steady stream of die-hard wave-chasers. The real attraction is the village's laid-back and friendly atmosphere, its simple way of life, and perhaps best of all, the wonderful feeling of being a long way away from anywhere else.

40

There is a range of interesting excursions on offer here, including boat trips to the nearby Pottuvil Lagoon, 'sea safaris' in search of dolphins and other marine life and cycling tours of local villages.

Around 15km (9 miles) down the main road heading inland from Arugam Bay is the small but beautiful **Lahugala National Park** (daily 6.30am– 6.30pm; currently free), and the scenic tropical dry forest that surrounds it. Lahugala is home to a large number of elephants, which congregate around the picturesque Lahugala Tank.

Palm trees line the coast

THE NORTH

The north is Sri Lanka's least known and least developed region. Out of bounds during the two decades of civil war, the area is only gradually reopening to visitors after the end of the civil war in 2009 and remains almost completely untouched by modern tourism. Not that the region is without attractions. Home to an almost exclusively Tamil population, the north is quite unlike the rest of Sri Lanka, and its long history has blended Hindu, Christian and colonial traditions into a unique whole.

Jaffna

For visitors accustomed to the Sinhalese south, the historic old Tamil city of **Jaffna** offers an entirely different perspective on Sri Lanka. The crucible of Tamil culture on the island, the city looks for inspiration as much to India, a short distance north over the Palk Straits, as to Colombo, and retains a character quite different from that in the rest of the island. Repeatedly besieged and fought over during the civil war, parts of Jaffna still bear the signs of conflict, most notably in the area around the huge Dutch fort, the largest in Asia. Much of the city, however, has survived surprisingly intact. The town centre remains vibrant and colourful, dotted with expansive Hindu temples and huge churches, and in the suburbs, decaying old Dutch villas still line the sedate, tree-lined streets. On the northern edge of town, the majestic **Nallur Kandaswamy Temple** is the most majestic Hindu temple in Sri Lanka, and the only one which rivals the great temples of India in size and in the intensity of its religious rituals and festivals.

The Jaffna Peninsula and Islands

Surrounding Jaffna at the northernmost point of Sri Lanka, the **Jaffna Peninsula** was for centuries the breadbasket of

Jaffna street scene

Jaffna city. Densely populated and agriculturally fertile, the peninsula has long been intensively settled, and is home to a cluster of low-key but interesting sights, ranging from the war-damaged temples of **Naguleswaram** and **Mavidddapuram**; the hot springs of **Keerimalai**; the ancient cluster of miniature stupas at **Kantharoadai**; the village of **Velvettiturai** ('VVT'), birthplace of the infamous LTTE supremo Prabakaran; and the remarkable sand dunes of the **Manalkadu Desert**; as well as a smattering of little-visited beaches.

East of Jaffna, the shallow waters of the Jaffna lagoon are dotted with a string of beautiful islands, on which can be found further mementos of the region's long and intriguing history, including the Dutch forts of Urundi and Hammenhiel at **Kayts**; the temples of **Nainativu**; and finally the remote outpost of **Delft**, home not only to an unusual population of wild ponies, but also to a colonial fort and even a rare African baobab tree, thought to have been planted by the Portuguese.

WHAT TO DO

SHOPPING

Sri Lanka isn't quite the shopper's paradise of nearby India, Thailand or Indonesia. The island does churn out a lot of handicrafts, but sadly much of it is poor-quality tourist tat, exemplified by the third-rate suitcase-fillers sold at the government-run Laksala chain, which has shops in all the main towns around the island. There is interesting stuff to be found, however, if you are prepared to hunt around. The best places are Colombo, Kandy and the west coast resorts. Bargaining is the order of the day in all places except in the smartest shops – a request for a 'small discount' or 'special price' can work in many situations, especially if you are buying several items or making a big purchase, while at the more informal little shops and stalls you can usually haggle to your heart's content.

Handicrafts and Souvenirs

The most characterful Sri Lankan souvenirs are the brightly painted masks which are sold all over the country, especially along the west coast – the best selection can be found at Ambalangoda, the centre of the island's mask-making industry. Size and quality vary enormously: from the minute to the huge, and from sloppily painted junk to meticulously crafted heirlooms. Elephant carvings are also ubiquitous, in wood, metal or stone, as well as elephant paintings and batiks, stuffed toy elephants, elephant jigsaws and so on. Again, quality varies widely. Next in popularity come Buddha carvings, in a similarly wide range of media and quality.

Bird batik, Aluvihara

A bright mask to lure tourists and frighten demons

Metalwork (a speciality of the Kandy area) is popular, though the island's trays, candlesticks, plates and carvings can be a bit ornate for western tastes. Batik painting (introduced by the Dutch from Indonesia) is also fairly common. Most pieces feature tropical beach scenes, elephants or the Sigiriya Damsels, though a few places turn out more unusual stuff. Reasonable leatherwork and lacquerware is also available in a few places.

For something more unusual you could look out for Kandyan drums, carrom boards or religious kitsch, such as the colourful posters of Hindu and Buddhist gods, which are sold all over the island.

Finally, a number of shops in Colombo offer chic contemporary takes on traditional handicrafts. Places to try include Paradise Road, the shop at the Gallery Café and, best of all, the celebrated Barefoot, whose signature hand-woven cottons and linens are used in the making of a wide selection

Tea and Spices

There is plenty of tea for sale in Sri Lanka, either in dedicated tea shops (Mlesna is the main chain) or in general shops and supermarkets (Cargills supermarkets usually have a good stock), though the range is often fairly limited. You might also want to stock up on cheap spices from local shops – though spices sold in the island's myriad spice gardens are usually massively marked up.

of vibrantly coloured objects, from clothes and tablecloths to fabric-covered stationery and unusual cuddly toys.

Gems and Jewellery

Sri Lanka's fame as a major international source of high-quality precious stones is reflected in the large number of gem and jewellery shops which dot the island's major tourist haunts. Shopping around may turn up some modest bargains, though unless you are an expert gemologist, stick to reputable shops and make sure you have done your homework so that you are able to compare prices and quality in Sri Lanka with those in your home country.

Needless to say, buying gems from touts or street traders (such as those who hang around Ratnapura, the island's main gem-producing centre) is asking for trouble unless you really know your stuff.

A jeweller inspects gems at the moonstone mines, Mitiyagoda

ENTERTAINMENT

Sri Lanka is badly lacking in nightlife. The island's only established nightclubs are found exclusively in Colombo – all are attached to big hotels but none is particularly special. It's probably better to head to one of the city's handful of bars, pubs and live-music venues, all of which can stay lively till late.

The liveliest places on the coast are Hikkaduwa and Unawatuna, though even here things are pretty sleepy – quiet late-night beers on the beach and Bob Marley are the order of the day (or night) here, although there are occasional beach parties, plus an annual beach festival in Hikkaduwa held in July/August. Negombo also boasts a few lively bars in season, but away from these places, you can pretty much forget it.

Kandyan dance performers

After-hours entertainment is also largely non-existent. Colombo has a couple of cinemas and a smattering of cultural events, but that is about it. In Kandy, be sure to sample one of the shows of Kandyan dancing and drumming which are staged nightly at various venues around town (usually in the larger hotels) – all are thoroughly touristy but undeniably fun, with acrobatic dancing, exuberant drumming and fire-walking guaranteed.

Cricket practice on the beach

SPORTS AND RELAXATION

Cricket

As in India and Pakistan, cricket is a national obsession in Sri Lanka – it is impossible to go far without seeing kids playing games with improvised bats and balls on any available bit of space, and matches featuring the national team are followed religiously by virtually every man and boy on the island. Test matches and one-day internationals are held in Colombo, Kandy and Galle, while Dambulla also hosts one-day internationals.

Golf

Increasing numbers of tourists are taking advantage of the island's three beautiful 18-hole golf courses (all over 5,460m or 6,000yds; par 70–73), which can be found in Colombo, Kandy and Nuwara Eliya – the last two are particularly scenic. All three courses welcome casual visitors, and green fees and club hire are an absolute bargain compared with most other courses around the world.

Swimming

Splashing around into the warm waters of the Indian Ocean is one of the great pleasures of a visit to Sri Lanka. But swimming conditions vary enormously around the coast, even within quite small distances along individual beaches, and there are strong currents and undertows in places, so it is always worth seeking local advice if you want to swim off a deserted section of beach – a depressing number of Sri Lankans drown every year, as well as the occasional tourist. Be very careful if you are on the coast during the monsoon when seas can be rough. Most larger hotels have a swimming pool which can generally be used by non-guests for a fee.

Diving

Although not on a par with the nearby Maldives, Sri Lanka has a good range of diving sites and a well-established network of PADI diving schools around most parts of the coast. The island's marine environment is far from pristine, especially on the west coast, but although many of the offshore reefs have suffered significant damage, the coastal waters still boast abundant marine life, interesting underwater rock and cave formations and (on the west and south coasts) a large number of rewarding wreck dives. Most of the island's diving schools are situated on the west coast, mainly in the Bentota area and at Hikkaduwa, and there are also schools on the south coast at Unawatuna, Weligama and Tangalla.

Diving dates

The diving season runs from November to April on the west and south coasts, and from May to October on the east coast.

Surfing at Midigama on the south coast

Snorkelling

There is very little good snorkelling in Sri Lanka, and most of the reefs close to the shore have been seriously damaged. The best spots are at Pigeon Island, at Nilaveli on the east coast, and at Polhena on the south coast (which has the added bonus of a couple of expert local snorkelling guides, contactable via the village's guesthouses). The Coral Gardens in Hikkaduwa also offer decent snorkelling and plenty of tropical fish, but are rather spoilt for snorkellers by the number of boats riding around.

Surfing

There are several excellent surf spots around the Sri Lankan coast. The island's premier surfing destination is Arugam Bay, which is internationally famous for its waves (best from May to October), offering a variety of breaks suitable for all standards from novice to expert. The other two main surfing destinations are Midigama on the south coast, and Hikkaduwa on the west coast (both best from November to April). There are specialist surfing shops at Arugam Bay and Hikkaduwa which offer tuition, board rental and repairs, and which also organise surf safaris to breaks along the coast.

Other Watersports

The water sports capital is Bentota, where the placid waters of the Bentota lagoon provide the perfect spot for all sorts of water-based fun, including windsurfing, water-skiing, jet-skiing, speed-boating, banana-boating, tube-riding, kayaking and lagoon boat trips (all of which can be organised through the resort's myriad water sports centres).

The best spot for white-water rafting is Kitulgala, on the southwestern edge of the hill country, where the choppy Kelani Ganga river (famous as the location for the film *The Bridge on the River Kwai*) provides boulder-strewn stretches of grade 3–4 rapids.

Trekking and Cycling

The island's vast potential for activity holidays remains largely unexploited, though things are slowly changing. The hill country, in particular, is a walkers' paradise, with stunning scenery and a pleasantly temperate climate, though the lack of established long-distance hiking trails means that it's best to sign up with a local tour operator rather than attempting to strike out on your own.

Cyclists have thousands of miles of relatively traffic-free minor roads to explore, though again it's probably easiest to take a tour with an established local operator – Adventure Asia and Jetwing Eco-Holidays *(see pages 122–3)* are the two best for both hiking and cycling, as well as other activity holidays.

Wildlife

Sri Lanka has an outstanding collection of national parks covering large swathes of the island and boasting a fascinating array of wildlife. For most visitors the main attraction is the elephants, which can be seen in almost all the island's national parks, while the island's superb leopards are also a major draw, most easily seen at Yala National Park, which has one of the world's highest concentrations of this elusive mammal. Various species of monkey, sloth bears, several types of deer, buffalo, wild boar, assorted squirrels, crocodiles and large monitor lizards are also commonly spotted here.

A leopard in Yala National Park

Sri Lanka is also one of Asia's premier bird-watching locations, boasting a vast range of colourful avifauna. The island's wide range of natural habitats – from coastal wetlands to cloud forest – supports a uniquely varied array of resident bird life, while its equatorial location also attracts a wide range of seasonal migrants from as far away as Europe. More than 230 resident species have been recorded, including 33 endemic species which are found only on the island.

Whale-Watching and Turtle-Watches

Over the past few year's, Sri Lanka has emerged as a leading whale-watching destination (best from November to April).

The main centre for trips is the village of Mirissa, near the southern point of the island. Blue whales are the most commonly spotted species, while sperm whales are sighted with reasonable frequency.

The island is also an important turtle-nesting site, with five different species of marine turtle visiting the island. Turtle watches are run nightly on the beach at Rekawa, near Tangalla, and at Kosgoda, near Bentota. Sightings are most common from January to May (usually reaching a peak in April), particularly during nights on or around the full moon.

Yoga and Meditation

Yoga courses and facilities are less well established in Sri Lanka than in neighbouring India, although increasing numbers of ayurveda centres now offer yoga sessions either on their own or as part of treatment courses. Aficionados might consider a visit to Ulpotha (www.ulpotha.com), a specialist yoga retreat in the Cultural Triangle which attracts top international teachers for its two-week residential courses, though at top international prices.

The best place to study meditation is Kandy, which has a number of well-established centres. The best for foreign visitors is the Nilambe Meditation Centre (tel: 0777-804 555; www.nilambe.org), in a beautiful setting high in the hills about 20km (12 miles) outside the city.

Ayurveda

The traditional system of holistic health care known as Ayurveda (from the Sanskrit, meaning 'the science of life') has been practised in India and Sri Lanka for centuries. According to the Ayurvedic system, all bodies are made up of varying combinations of the five basic elements (ether, fire, air, earth and water) and governed by three *doshas* (*pitta*, *vata* and *kapha*), each of which is a combination of two or three of the five elements. Illnesses are seen simply as the result of an imbalance in the *doshas*, and so rather than treating illnesses and symptoms in isolation, Ayurveda aims to treat the whole patient, often trying to encourage a more balanced lifestyle.

A huge number of places (mainly in the west coast resorts) now offer Ayurveda treatments. These are basically of two types. Serious Ayurveda resorts and clinics cater for visitors (often with chronic medical problems) who go for long-term courses of treatment. Far more common, however, are so-called 'soft' Ayurveda treatments, most commonly various forms of massage, herbal and steam baths, and *shirodhara*, which involves dribbling hot oil on the forehead (or 'third eye'). Although they are extremely pleasurable, these are essentially glorified de-stress and beauty treatments rather than genuine medical therapies. The massive boom in 'soft' Ayurveda over the past decade has recently encouraged many of the smarter west-coast hotels to open sumptuous new spas, in which 'soft' Ayurveda treatments are offered alongside mainstream spa treatments such as wraps and body-polishes, facials, reflexology and aromatherapy treatments, and various forms of international-style massages such as Thai and Swedish.

An energy-giving *marma* scrub

CHILDREN'S SRI LANKA

The beach is likely to provide the main entertainment for kids visiting Sri Lanka, with mile upon mile of golden sand to play around on and warm waters to dip into – though parents should always check local swimming conditions *(see page 92)* and be attentive to the very real dangers of sunburn and dehydration.

Away from the coast, the country's top children's attraction is the Elephant Orphanage at Pinnewala, whose elephants are a guaranteed hit, especially the tiny babies – one of the very few places in the world where kids can see elephants which are even smaller than themselves. A rattling jeep ride around any of the island's other national parks in search of elephants, leopards or other wildlife is also fun.

Older kids will enjoy some of the island's activity sports, such as water sports at Bentota or white-water rafting at Kitulgala *(see page 94)*. All levels of rafting are available from here. A tuktuk ride, a train trip through the hill country or a boat trip on one of the island's rivers or lagoons, or even in a fishing boat along the coast, should also appeal, while those with a head for heights might also fancy the challenge of clambering up Sigiriya.

Ball games on the beach

Finally, there are plenty of gruesome masks, painted elephants and wooden toys on sale all over the island – and if you are in Colombo, be sure to bag a colourful cuddly animal or two from Barefoot *(see page 88)* before you leave.

FESTIVALS

It is sometimes said that Sri Lanka has more festivals than any other country in the world, and with 25 public holidays a year plus numerous festivals (lasting up to a month) from four different religions, it is easy to believe. The calendar on *page 100* gives only the most important of the country's innumerable celebrations.

Virtually all the island's major festivals are religious in inspiration, and many centre around elaborate night-time processions, or *peraheras*, featuring lots of exquisitely dressed elephants, dancers and drummers. Many festivals occur on *poya* (full-moon) days, which are held to be sacred by Buddhists who traditionally retire to their temples to meditate and pray for the day. Most festivals follow the Buddhist lunar calendar, so dates vary slightly from year to year. For a complete listing of events and exact dates, visit www.srilanka.travel.

The Esala Perahera

Sri Lanka's most spectacular festival is the magnificent Esala Perahera, held in Kandy over the 10 days leading up to the Esala Poya in late July/early August (exact dates vary; check www.srilanka.travel). Held in honour of the city's revered Tooth Relic, the festival consists of a series of nightly processions around the city which gradually increase in scale and exuberance over the course of the 10 days. By the final few nights, the procession will have grown to mammoth proportions, with around a thousand dancers, drummers, fire-eaters and others, plus a hundred or so magnificently attired elephants, with a replica of the Tooth Relic carried on the back of the lead elephant, the so-called Maligawa Tusker – a vast explosion of noise, colour and religious pageantry without equal in Sri Lanka, or indeed anywhere else in Asia.

Festival Calendar

January *Duruthu Poya* commemorates the first of the Buddha's three legendary visits to the island with a spectacular procession at Kelaniya, just outside Colombo. On 14–15 January, the Hindu harvest festival of *Thai Pongol* is marked by ceremonies at Hindu temples across the island and the ceremonial cooking of newly garnered rice.

Late January/early February Launched in 2007, the Galle Literary Festival (www.galleliteraryfestival.com) is one of the biggest events of its kind in Asia, attracting leading writers from around the globe.

February *Navam Poya* is celebrated with a big elephant procession at Colombo's Gangaramaya temple – a relatively modern festival.

13–14 April The Buddhist and Hindu New Year (roughly coinciding with the west coast monsoon). Families swap gifts, *kiribath* (milk-cooked rice) cakes are eaten, new clothes worn and horoscopes cast.

Good Friday The island of Duwa hosts a major Easter Passion play

May The most important of Sri Lanka's *poya* days, *Vesak* combines a three-fold celebration of the Buddha's birth, enlightenment and death (all of which are traditionally believed to have occurred on this one day). Devout Buddhists visit their temple to meditate, free food is given out at the roadside and lamps are lit in front of houses.

June–August *Poson Poya*, the second most important of Sri Lanka's poya days, celebrates the introduction of Buddhism to the island by Mahinda, with pilgrims congregating on Anuradhapura and Mihintale.

July The lunar month of Esala is Sri Lanka's festival season. The most famous is Esala Perahera at Kandy *(see page 99)*, while there are also major festivals at Kataragama and Dondra.

August Honouring the god Skanda, *Vel* is one of the island's most important Hindu festivals, with colourful processions in Colombo during which the god's chariot is dragged across the city.

Late October/early November *Deepavali* is the Sri Lankan equivalent to North India's Diwali, celebrating the exploits of Rama and the triumph of good over evil.

25 December Christmas.

EATING OUT

Sri Lankan cooking is a lot like the island itself: a unique fusion of Indian, Asian and European influences which have been mixed together over the centuries to produce a highly flavoured and hugely enjoyable cuisine quite unlike any other. Rice and curry remains the national staple, though this plain name completely fails to describe the culinary magnificence of the best Sri Lankan cooking, while there are lots of intriguingly named local specialities to sample – *hoppers*, *string hoppers*, *lamprais*, *pittu*, *kottu rotty* and *watalappan*, to name just a few.

Central to the island's unique cuisine is its own distinctive local produce and its vast array of spices – Sri Lankan cooking is typically hot (and often downright fiery), with crisp chilli and coconut flavours which are often more reminiscent than Thai cooking than Indian. Adding to the heat are the distinctive local *sambols*, a kind of Sri Lankan salt and pepper, which are served as condiments – and you will probably come across the ubiquitous *pol sambol*, a bland-looking but palate-scorching combination of finely grated coconut and chilli. Approach with caution.

Dried chillies

Tempting vegetarian dishes

WHERE TO EAT

The main problem with Sri Lankan food is finding really good places to sample it: too many places, from the big west-coast resorts to smaller hotels and guesthouses around the island, offer up lame international tourist standards or tired buffets which give no hint of the island's wonderful cuisine – and, except in Colombo, decent independent restaurants are disappointingly thin on the ground. Having said that, there are a reasonable number of good places if you know where to look. A lot of the island's best restaurants are located in top-end hotels, some of which offer excellent cooking in luxurious surroundings. At the other end of the spectrum you will sometimes find excellent home cooking at relatively modest little guesthouses – a great opportunity for tourists to enjoy proper Sri Lankan home cooking at bargain prices.

Anywhere with even the slightest tourist pretensions will have an English-language menu – although wild variations in spelling can sometimes make it tricky to work out what is being offered. In the unlikely event that you end up eating in a local café you will just have to point at whatever food is on the counter or at what other diners are eating – though there will probably only be one or two choices available in any case.

WHAT TO EAT

Rice and Curry

Sri Lanka's national dish is rice and curry, a term which covers everything from the basic meals served up in local cafés to the sumptuous banquets dished up in the island's top hotels and restaurants. The classic Sri Lankan rice and curry features a dozen or more dishes of contrasting ingredients and flavours served with an enormous mound of rice – more

Breakfast and Snacks

Rotis are rather dry pancakes made from onion batter, eaten for breakfast with *sambol*, butter or marmalade, or as a snack. The traditional Sri Lankan breakfast consists of pancakes called *hoppers* (crispy on the outside, soft inside). If there is an egg in the middle, it will be an egg hopper. String hoppers are tangled circles of steamed noodles, which when eaten with a meat curry taste delicious, even in the morning. *Kiribeth* is a type of milk rice, usually served with *jaggery*, a sweetener made from palm syrup. For a snack, call in at a roadside stall and try a vegetarian spring roll or *cutlis*, pockets of dough filled with cold chicken or fish. Be warned: the meatballs and round, often fish-filled rolls *(malu pan)* are fiendishly hot. One dessert is *wattalappam*, a coconut crème caramel. Curd is a yoghurt made from buffalo milk – try it with *jaggery*.

akin to a South Indian thali (or even Middle Eastern *meze* or Indonesian *rijstafel*) than a traditional North Indian curry.

The range of dishes varies from place to place but will usually feature a meat or fish curry, dhal and poppadums along with local favourites such as curried pineapple, caramelised aubergine, potato or sweet potato curry, curried green beans, *mallung* (shredded green vegetable fried with spices and coconut) and a range of *sambols*, as well as dishes using unusual local specialities such as drumsticks (similar to okra), curried jakfruit or ash plantain. The range is pretty much endless, and part of the fun of travelling around the island is in sampling different local variations on the island's national dish.

Making *rotty*

Rice and curry is undoubtedly king in the Sri Lankan cookbook, but there are plenty of other local specialities worth sampling (see 'Breakfasts and Snacks' on *page 103*). *Lamprais* is a mound of rice plus toppings (typically a lump of chicken, a boiled egg and some pickle) baked and served in a banana leaf – a kind of simplified local take on the North Indian biriani.

The most popular Muslim contribution to Sri Lankan cooking is the *rotty*, a doughy pancake (similar to a Malaysian *murtabak*) wrapped up in various shapes around spicy dollops of vegetable or potato. Alternatively, *rotty* is chopped up and stir-fried with meat and vegetable to produce *kottu rotty*, a popular evening snack usually cooked on the spot outside

local cafés by machete-wielding chefs – listen for the noise of furious chopping and banging. You might also come across *pittu*, a mix of grated coconut and flour steamed in a cylindrical bamboo mould, and you will definitely find 'devilled' dishes (devilled pork, chicken and beef are all common) – bite-size hunks of meat served in a delicious, moderately-spicy barbecue sauce with big chunks of tomato, onion and chilli.

Seafood

Around the coast, seafood also plays a big role in the Sri Lankan diet, with a wide range of freshly caught fish – tuna, seer, mullet and shark among them – plus cuttlefish *(calamari)*, crab and prawns (those from the Negombo lagoon are particularly prized). Fiery fish curries are common, as is chilli crab, though otherwise preparation is fairly simple and usually not too spicy, with the fish grilled, bread crumbed or served in a simple garlic sauce.

International Cuisines

Other cuisines have also established themselves in the island's culinary mainstream. Colombo boasts dozens of excellent little South Indian restaurants, unpretentious places dishing up subcontinental classics like *dosas* (crispy rice pancakes), *iddlis* (steamed rice cakes) and *vadais* (spicy doughnuts made from deep-fried lentil-flour) at giveaway prices. Chinese food is also ubiquitous. Though generally spiced up for local tastes with distinctly un-Chinese hunks of chilli, it is often tasty and cheap. And in Colombo a lot of restaurants serve up the full range of international cuisine, from Japanese and Thai to Italian and French, with varying degrees of authenticity.

Desserts

Sri Lanka also has a good range of desserts. The classic pudding is *curd*, a deliciously thick and creamy yoghurt made from buffalo milk, usually served with honey. You might also encounter *wattalappam*, an egg-based dessert from Malaysia which tastes a bit like crème caramel. *Kiribath*, rice cooked in milk, is traditionally served at weddings and other festivals. More mainstream puddings and snacks include a decent range of ice-cream (the Elephant House brand is ubiquitous) and colourful cakes, often made in lurid colours and with a faintly curried flavour, are also popular, especially in Kandy. South Indian restaurants in Colombo usually have a selection of classic Indian sweets such as *laddu* and *burfi*.

Fruits

Sri Lanka also boasts a wonderful array of tropical fruits. Bananas come in all shapes and sizes, from fat little yellow miniatures to huge red monsters. Pineapple, mango and papaya are all found everywhere, as are coconuts. The enormous jakfruit, the world's biggest fruit, is often served curried as part of a rice and curry, while *durian*, another massive fruit, is a reputed aphrodisiac – though its peculiarly smelly aroma makes it something of an acquired taste. *Mangosteens* look like purple tomatoes and hold a delicious fruit which tastes like a slightly citrus-flavoured grape. The outlandish-looking *rambutan* is covered in bright red tentacles, inside which is a delicately flavoured, lychee-like fruit. Wood apples – round, apple-sized fruits covered in a tough wooden

Fresh tropical fruit at the market

shell – are also common; crack them open to discover a red, rather bitter seed-filled flesh, usually served softened with a dash of honey.

WHAT TO DRINK

Tea in Sri Lanka is a bit of a disappointment – most of the island's best beverages get exported, meaning that you are unlikely to get more than a milky cup of tea-bag tea. There is also lots of locally grown coffee, which is usually quite palatable. International brands of fizzy drinks are available everywhere, though it is kinder to the local economy and your own teeth to stick to local brews. Ginger beer is a particular favourite, while there is also an interesting range of bizarre-tasting local fizzy pops to explore like Portello or Necta. Coconut milk is also available pretty much everywhere – look for men hanging around with a bunch of coconuts and a machete – and is claimed to be good for upset stomachs and hangovers alike thanks to its rich mix of glucose and potassium.

Sri Lankans love to drink, and the island isn't short of tipples both hard and soft. The nation's lager of choice is Lion Lager, followed by another local brew, Three Coins, and Carlsberg, brewed locally under licence. Imported wines are widely available at top-end hotels, though at a price, while a few bottles of rather strange-tasting Sri Lankan wines also occasionally make their way onto drinks lists. The island's top drink, however, is *arrack*, a feisty (33 percent proof) spirit made from refined toddy, tapped from coconut. Tasting a little like rum, *arrack* is available in various grades (double-distilled is easier on the palate and makes for softer hangovers). It can be drunk neat, mixed with coke or lemonade, or used as a base for all sorts of cocktails.

Stuffed *rotty* and tea for breakfast

MENU READER

ash plantain	Sri Lankan plantain, often used in curries
cuttlefish	calamari
dosa	crispy rice pancake
drumsticks	Sri Lankan vegetable, similar to okra
hopper	small pancake served on its own or with various ingredients cooked inside
iddli	steamed rice cake
lamprais	rice plus toppings (chicken, egg and pickle) served in a banana leaf
mallung	shredded green vegetables fried with spices and coconut
kottu rotty	rotty chopped up and stir-fried with meat and/or vegetables
pittu	a mix of grated coconut and flour steamed in a bamboo mould
rotty	a doughy pancake wrapped around spicy dollops of vegetable or potato
string hoppers	small roundels of fine rice noodles
sambols	spicy relishes served with curries
vadais	spicy doughnuts made from deep-fried lentil-flour

Desserts

curd	creamy yogurt made from buffalo milk
kiribath	rice cooked in milk
wattalappam	egg-based dessert, like crème caramel

Drinks

arrack	popular Sri Lankan spirit, similar to rum and made from refined toddy
thambili	coconut milk
toddy	alcoholic drink made from coconut sap

PLACES TO EAT

We have used the following symbols to give an idea of the price for a three-course meal for one, including wine, cover and service:

$$$ over $12 $$ $6–12 $ below $6

COLOMBO

Barefoot Cafe $ *706 Galle Road, Colombo 3, tel: 011-258 0114.* Set in the beautiful courtyard at the back of Colombo's finest shop, this little urban oasis offers unpretentious but well-prepared café-standards including sandwiches, pasta dishes and good daily specials, as well as juices, milkshakes and moreish puddings. Daily until 7pm (Sun until 4pm).

Chesa Swiss $$$ *3 Deal Place, Colombo 3, tel: 011-257 3433.* Swiss-owned restaurant in a lovely colonial villa whose consistently good food draws a faithful expat clientele. Classic Swiss dishes (fondues, rosti, barley soup) share menu space with prime Australian steaks, seafood and vegetarian dishes. Only open in the evening.

Cricket Club Cafe $$ *34 Queens Road, Colombo 3, tel: 011-250 1384.* One of Colombo's most popular eating and drinking haunts, this cricket-themed café has walls plastered with photos, scorecards and signed bats, and a simple but tasty selection of burgers, stir fries, pasta dishes, steaks and daily specials. The cosy little pub-style bar gets lively with expats and tourists after dark.

Curry Leaf $$$ *Hilton Hotel, 2 Sir Chittampalam A. Gardiner Mawatha, Colombo 2, tel: 011-249 2492.* The jungle village decor at this outdoor restaurant may be a bit cheesy, but the nightly Sri Lankan buffet is one of the city's best places to introduce yourself to the island's culinary delights, from string hoppers to *wattalapan*, plus oodles of rice and curry. Only open in the evening.

Gallery Café $$ *2 Alfred House Road, Colombo 3, tel: 011-258 2162.* This ultra-chic courtyard café is set in a wonderfully stylish building designed by Geoffrey Bawa, who used to have his office here. There is decent food from an international menu, or just go for a coffee and the chance to rub shoulders with Colombo's smart set.

Greenlands $ *Shrubbery Gardens, Colombo 4.* A Colombo institution, this perennially popular restaurant serves up generous portions of top-notch South Indian vegetarian cooking at giveaway prices. The menu features *dosas*, *iddlis* and *vadais* galore, and if you've still got room afterwards there is a huge glass cabinet filled with colourful South Indian sweets at the entrance.

The Mango Tree $$ *82 Dharmapala Mawatha, tel: 011-587 9790.* One of the best Indian restaurants in town, drawing a loyal local clientele thanks to its wide-ranging and well-prepared selection of north Indian-style meat, seafood and vegetarian dishes, including hearty tandooris, tikkas and kebabs.

Tao $$$ *Cinnamon Grand Hotel, 77 Galle Road, Colombo 3, tel: 011-249 7369.* In a memorable location amidst the palm-studded gardens of the Cinnamon Grand, Tao is one of Colombo's culinary highlights, with inventive meat and seafood fusion cuisine mixing Asian and European influences. Open evenings only.

THE WEST COAST

Bijou $$ *44 Porutota Road, Negombo, tel: 031-531 9577.* Swiss-owned restaurant with a homely pine interior and an excellently prepared selection of Swiss and central European dishes (fondues, steaks and pasta), as well as some of the best seafood in Negombo.

Lords $$$ *Porutota Road, Negombo.* Sleek modern bar-restaurant with stylish decor and a beautifully presented selection of international cuisine ranging from fish and chips to more unusual offerings such as cashew nut and raisin curry.

Refresh $$ *384 Galle Road, Hikkaduwa, tel: 091-227 7810.* Attractive beachside restaurant with perhaps the fattest menu on the island, featuring a vast array of local and international cuisine – anything from *gazpacho* to *gado-gado*.

Sands $$$ *The Beach Hotel, Negombo, tel: 031-227 3500.* The beachside restaurant at Negombo's top hotel provides a romantic setting for a range of excellently prepared international dishes, including a good selection of authentic Sri Lankan curries.

THE SOUTH COAST

Galle Fort Hotel $$$ *28 Church Street, Galle Fort, tel: 091-223 2870.* The food at this stunning hotel is some of the best non-Sri Lankan cooking you will find on the island, with the emphasis on fresh seafood and light, delicately flavoured Australian-style Southeast Asian food. Try either the lavish evening set menus (around $30 for 4–5 courses) or the more casual lunch and snack menu. Sit down with a coffee on the beautiful street-facing veranda.

Kingfisher $ *Unawatuna.* The best of the long string of informal café-restaurants lined up along Unawatuna beach, with beautiful views of the waves from its neat little terrace, excellent international food and a hypnotic chill-out soundtrack.

The Sun House $$$ *18 Upper Dickson Road, tel: 091-438 0275.* Even if you are not staying here, it's worth the walk up the hill for an evening meal at this superb little boutique hotel. The setting in an old colonial villa is incomparably romantic, and the food, featuring a daily-changing set menu of three-course dinners showcasing the very best of Sri Lankan and Indian Ocean cuisine is likely to be amongst the very best you will find on the island. Book before 1pm for dinner.

KANDY

Devon Restaurant $ *11 Dalada Vidiya.* The decor at this functional modern restaurant won't win any awards but the food is cheap, tasty and unpretentious. Choose from an extensive menu featuring *burianis*, *lamprais*, noodles, devilled dishes and lots more, as well as tasty hoppers for breakfast.

The Pub $$ *36 Dalada Vidiya*. Right in the middle of town, with seating either in the modern interior or outside on the superb little terrace above the street (arrive early to secure a table). Food touristy but reasonably well prepared, with international dishes ranging from pasta and pork chops through to seafood and curries.

THE HILL COUNTRY

The Hill Club $$$ *Off Grand Hotel Road, tel: 052-222 2653.* Sample a real taste of the colonial life of yesteryear. The food itself is pretty average, but the real attraction is the time-warped colonial aura of the evening meal, served by white-gloved waiters in the chintzy dining room. It's all strangely compelling and decidedly formal. Men are only admitted if clad in the obligatory jacket and tie (though these are available free at the club if you don't have your own).

King Prawn $$ *Glendower Hotel, Grand Hotel Road, tel: 052-222 2501.* The food at this cosy little restaurant is about as authentic as Chinese cooking gets in Sri Lanka, although still with enough spice to keep the hill-country chills at bay.

Old Course Restaurant $$$ *St Andrew's Hotel, 10 St Andrew's Drive, tel: 052-222 3031.* The atmospheric oak-panelled restaurant at Nuwara Eliya's smartest hotel offers a homely setting for top-notch local and international cuisine, accompanied by one of the island's biggest wine lists.

THE EAST

Siam View Hotel $ *Arugam Bay, tel: 063-224 8195.* This popular guesthouse is home to a wooden Thai-style restaurant complete with genuine resident Thai chef who prepares a range of spicy curries and other southeast Asian dishes. This restaurant is a surprising but very welcome feature of the remote east-coast surfers' village of Arugam Bay.

A–Z TRAVEL TIPS

A Summary of Practical Information

A

ACCOMMODATION (see also CAMPING and RECOMMENDED HOTELS on page 133)

Sri Lanka has a vast range of accommodation in all price brackets, from ultra-basic $10-a-night guesthouses to luxurious $1,000-a-night boutique hotels and villas. Wherever there are tourists you will find accommodation, usually a surprisingly wide range, and the explosion in upmarket accommodation over the past few years means that if you have got a bit of money, you can enjoy top-notch style and comforts at relatively affordable prices. Some of Sri Lanka's top hotels and guesthouses are almost attractions in their own right, and there is a plethora of romantic colonial-era properties and stylish modern hotels (exemplified by the island's superb string of Geoffrey Bawa-designed hotels, such as the Jetwing Lighthouse and Heritance Kandalama – *see pages 137 and 141*) as well as more unusual offerings, whether you are looking for the chance to stay in a converted tea factory or a natural cave.

Simple guesthouses can be found all over the island, usually family-run affairs either in private houses or small-scale custom-built lodgings. Many offer excellent value for money, with comfortable rooms and good home cooking for $25 per night for a double, or less. Hotels come in all shapes and sizes, from simple business and tourist hotels ($50–75 a night), package tourist-oriented resort hotels ($100–150 a night) mainly found along the west coast, to five-star palaces in stunning modern or colonial properties (anything from $200 and upwards per night). There is also an ever-increasing number of luxury villas available for hire, usually lovingly restored colonial properties with bags of character – there's a good selection of properties on www.villasinsrilanka.com, www.boutiquesrilanka.com, www.srilankainstyle.com and www.reddottours.com.

Because of the large number of beds available it is almost never a problem finding a room, except at the very busiest times, though there is no harm in ringing or emailing ahead to reserve a room. The smaller and more exclusive the hotel, the more you are advised to book in advance, though it is usually fine to just turn up and take your chances at simple guesthouses. Prices in coastal areas fluctuate seasonally. Prices go up by anything from 10 to 50 percent during the season (November to April on the west coast; May to September on the east coast). Big festivals can also push prices through the roof, especially in Kandy during the Esala Perahera, or in Nuwara Eliya over Sinhalese New Year in April.

Note that there are no youth hostels in Sri Lanka.

AIRPORTS

Bandaranaike International Airport (CMB; www.airport.lk) is located at Katunayake, 30km (19 miles) north of Colombo and 10km (6 miles) south of Negombo. There are plenty of unmetered taxis and touts hanging around: agree the fare in advance and count on around Rs.3,000 to Colombo (1hr), Rs.1,500 to Negombo (20min), or Rs.7,000 to Kandy (3hr). There are also shuttle buses every half hour to the nearby Averiwatte bus station, from where you can pick up onward services to Colombo, Kandy and Negombo.

The only other commercial airport is at Ratmalana, in the southern suburbs of Colombo near Mount Lavinia, from where a couple of local operators run internal flights to Jaffna (1hr) and Trincomalee (1hr).

B

BICYCLE AND MOTORBIKE HIRE

The bicycle remains the staple form of transport for most Sri Lankans, and many guesthouses offer bikes for hire – anything from rusty old sit-up-and-beg antiques to state-of-the-art mountain bikes (from Rs.100–1,000 per day). If your guesthouse cannot help you, asking around the village or town where you are staying will usually turn up something.

Motorbike hire is also available in a number of coastal resorts – Negombo and Hikkaduwa both have a couple of places renting out machines of various sizes, while you might also find bikes for hire elsewhere around the coast. Rates are generally very good value; a 250cc bike, for example, will usually cost around $10 per day.

BUDGETING FOR YOUR TRIP

Despite rampant inflation and significant price rises in recent years, Sri Lanka is still one of the cheaper countries in Asia to visit. How much you spend is really up to you: it is possible to scrape by on $20 a day by bedding down in a basic guesthouse and lolling on the beach. Equally, you could spend 50 times as much as this staying in the island's smartest hotels and availing yourself of the very best the island has to offer. As a rule of thumb, $100 per couple per day will get you acceptable accommodation and food and a reasonable range of tourist activities. For $200 per couple per day you can enjoy good mid- to upper-range accommodation and food and plenty of excursions. Staying in one of the island's luxury hotels or villas, however, will bump this figure up considerably.

Transport on buses and trains is so cheap as to be almost free – you could travel from one end of the island to another for under $25. A car and driver will set you back $40–60 per day, depending on the quality of the vehicle and who you arrange it through. A filling meal can cost from $1 in a local cafe to $75 in a top restaurant, including drinks. A big bottle of local beer usually will cost around $2.

Big recent price hikes in entrance fees at tourist attractions can put a strain on budget travellers' finances; there's a minimum fee of $5 at most museums, considerably more at major attractions ($20 at Pinnewala Elephant Orphanage, and $10 at the Temple of the Tooth, for example). It's also worth being aware of the punitive fees levied on foreigners visiting government-run national parks ($40 and more once you have paid for transport) and archaeological sites in the Cultural Triangle ($25).

C

CAMPING

Sri Lanka's only officially recognised campsites are in the island's national parks, although (ironically) camping in a national park (once you have factored in all the absurdly inflated fees which are levied on foreign visitors, plus the cost of transport and a driver) actually works out considerably more expensive than staying in even a mid-range hotel. If you are determined to experience a night under canvas in the wilds, various operators can fix you up with a guide, driver and all the necessary camping kit.

CAR HIRE *(see also Driving)*

The often chaotic local traffic and anarchic driving styles mean that few visitors drive themselves, although hiring a car with driver is a popular option. This can work out reasonably cheap, with rates from as little as $40 per day, depending on the length of the hire period and the mileage to be covered, and is well worth it to avoid the stress of having to deal with public transport and make the most of your stay. This can be arranged pretty much anywhere on the island, either through one of the tour operators listed on page 122, through a local operator like Malkey (www.malkey.lk) or Quickshaws (www.quickshaws.com) or through your guesthouse. Even places off the beaten track usually have local taxi drivers who will be happy to put themselves at your service for a day or for longer trips. For self-drive cars, Malkey is probably your best option. There are no nationwide breakdown services in Sri Lanka. Check with your car-hire firm before leaving what the procedure is should your vehicle cease working.

CLIMATE

Sri Lanka's climate is surprisingly complicated, with different weather patterns affecting different parts of the island. The welcome news is that there is always good weather in some part of the island at any time of year. The best time to visit the west and southwest coasts is from November to April; during the rest of the year the southwest (Yala) monsoon brings significant rainfall, with periodic deluges and overcast skies. The situation on the east coast is more or less exactly the opposite, the best time to visit being from April to September; from October to February the northeast (Maha) monsoon brings considerable rain and unsettled conditions to this side of the island. The hill country receives rain from both monsoons, particularly the Yala monsoon, which dumps huge quantities of rain on the southwest side of the hills. As such, the best time to visit the hills is from January to April. The Cultural Triangle sees little rain, although sporadic downpours caused by the northeast monsoon may be experienced from October to December. Temperatures are fairly constant year round, and are determined by altitude rather than by season, averaging around 27°C (81°F) on the coast, 22°C (72°F) in Kandy and just 16°C (61°F) in Nuwara Eliya.

	J	F	M	A	M	J	J	A	S	O	N	D
°C	5	6	10	13	19	21	23	22	20	14	8	6
°F	41	43	50	55	66	70	74	72	68	57	46	41

CLOTHING

As throughout South Asia, great importance is attached to personal appearance and cleanliness. Locals struggle to understand why visitors who can afford the airfare to Sri Lanka cannot also afford a decent set of clean clothes.

Skimpy beachwear is fine on the beach, though it is best to cover up (women especially) away from the sand, and toplessness and naturism are not permitted anywhere. When visiting Buddhist (and most Hindu) temples you should remove shoes and hats and cover shoulders and legs.

CRIME AND SAFETY

For visitors, Sri Lanka is a reassuringly safe and law-abiding country. Petty theft and pickpocketing are much less widespread than in many Asian countries, while violent crimes against tourists are very uncommon. Nevertheless, it is wise to take sensible precautions and don't invite trouble by leaving hotel rooms unlocked or valuables lying around. Women should avoid walking on their own along dark beaches (or other places) at night.

The major safety concern in Sri Lanka is traffic. The island has one of the world's highest rates of road fatalities. Keep your eyes and ears peeled whenever there is traffic around, and never expect vehicles to stop (or even slow down) when you are crossing the road.

Another major safety issue is swimming *(see page 92)*. Never swim in an isolated spot on your own and always seek local advice if there is no-one else swimming off a particular section of beach (strong currents and undertows are common).

The north and east of the island, until recently embroiled in civil war, are now safe to visit, although you should check the latest security situation carefully before attempting to visit these areas in case of further outbreaks of fighting or communal unrest.

D

DRIVING (see also Car Hire)

If you are determined to drive yourself, a few operators offer self-drive car hire, though this can actually work out more expensive than going with a driver. In order to hire a car you'll need an international driving licence (or your national driving licence plus a temporary driving permit from the Department of Motor Traffic in Boralesgamuwa, Colombo) Sri Lankans drive on the right and there's an official speed limit of 35mph in towns and 45mph outside, although given the crowded state of the roads, you'll be struggling to even reach these speeds.

E

ELECTRICITY

Most sockets require round, three-pin plugs. The current is 220–240V 50 cycles AC. Adaptors for all sorts of foreign plugs are widely available in hardware, electronic and phone shops everywhere.

EMBASSIES, CONSULATES AND HIGH COMMISSIONS

Australia: 21 Gregory's Road, Colombo 7, tel: 011-246 3200, www.srilanka.embassy.gov.au.

Canada: 33A, 5th Lane, Colombo 3, tel: 011-522 6232, www.canadainternational.gc.ca/sri_lanka.

Republic of Ireland: Honorary Consul, 35 Edward Lane, Colombo 3, tel: 011-258 7895.

United Kingdom: 389 Bauddhaloka Mawatha, Colombo 7, tel: 011-539 0639, http://ukinsrilanka.fco.gov.uk/en.

United States: 210 Galle Rd, Colombo 3, tel: 011-249 8500, http://srilanka.usembassy.gov.

EMERGENCIES

There are no national emergency telephone numbers in Sri Lanka. In a medical emergency your guesthouse/hotel manager should be able to put you in touch with a local English-speaking doctor.

G

GAY AND LESBIAN TRAVELLERS

Homosexuality is technically illegal in Sri Lanka, and although no-one has been convicted since the 1950s, the entire subject remains little understood by the majority of Sri Lankans and almost completely taboo. Discretion is advised. For information on the very secretive local scene, visit www.equal-ground.org or check out the various links at www.utopia-asia.com/tipssri.htm.

GETTING THERE

The only way to reach Sri Lanka at present is by air – ferry services from India were discontinued at the beginning of the civil war in 1983 and are unlikely to resume for the foreseeable future. The island is well connected to international air networks. There are direct flights from London with SriLankan Airlines and BMI, and numerous one-stop routings, most conveniently via India with Jet Airways, via the Gulf with Emirates, Gulf Air, Qatar Airlines, Kuwait Airlines Oman Air and Etihad, or via Asia with Thai Airways, Malaysia Airlines and Singapore Airlines.

There are no direct flights to the island from Ireland, North America or Australasia. Travelling from Ireland or the east coast of the US and Canada there are numerous convenient one- or two-stop routings via London or other European or Gulf cities. From the west coast of the US and Canada there is a similarly wide range of one- or two-stop flights via Asian hubs including Hong Kong, Singapore, Bangkok and Kuala Lumpur.

Sri Lanka is well connected with many other Asian cities. SriLankan Airlines flies directly to six destinations in India, including Delhi and Mumbai, as well as to all the Asian hub cities listed above.

GUIDES AND TOURS

There are hundreds of tour agencies and guides around the country, of wildly varying standards. The following are the best established operators, often boasting a degree of local expertise and knowledge.

Adventure Asia tel: 011-586 8468, www.ad-asia.com. Leading outdoor adventure specialists, offering a range of biking, climbing, rafting and kayaking trips, plus spectacular balloon flights over the Cultural Triangle.

Aitken Spence Travels tel: 011-230 8308, www.aitkenspence-travels.com. Travel arm of one of the island's leading hotel chains, offering a good mix of general island tours, plus wildlife and nature tours and Ayurveda packages.

Jetwing Travels tel: 011-234 5700, www.jetwingtravels.com. Professionally run island-wide tours run by the travel wing of Sri Lanka's largest hotel group with a mix of nature, culture and adventure themes.

Jetwing Eco-Holidays tel: 011-238 1201, www.jetwingeco.com. Sri Lanka's premier eco-tourism operator, with an outstanding range of wildlife activities led by a team of expert guides.

Walkers Tours tel: 011-230 6480, www.walkerstours.com. Reputable larger tour operators, offering general island-wide tours plus mountain-biking, trekking, bird watching, rafting, golf, watersports and diving packages.

H

HEALTH AND MEDICAL CARE

Immunisations are recommended for diphtheria, tetanus, hepatitis A and polio; you might also consider having yourself vaccinated for tuberculosis, meningitis and typhoid. Malaria is found in most parts of the island except in the hills and parts of the west and south coasts – consult your doctor about which course of prophylaxis would work best for you. The most effective way of avoiding malaria is, of course, to avoid being bitten in the first place. Take plenty of mosquito repellent and cover up with light-coloured clothing from dusk onwards.

Although tap water in Sri Lanka is chlorinated and technically safe to drink, it is best to stick to bottled or boiled water. Cases of mild diarrhoea caused by unsanitary food are much less common than in neighbouring India, but if you are unlucky enough to be struck down, drink lots of water to avoid dehydration and stick to bland foods like rice, yoghurt and bananas. Coconut milk is a good and safe source of liquid and contains valuable minerals such as potassium. If you have persistent severe diarrhoea, have a stool test to check for giardiasis and amoebic dysentery, both of which will require a course of antibiotics.

Standards of health care are reasonable; there are public hospitals in all major cities, plus numerous smaller private clinics. If you require treatment, the best first step is to ask at your hotel or guesthouse – any good establishment will be able to arrange for you to see an English-speaking doctor or to be taken to a reputable clinic. Health insurance is strongly recommended. All larger towns have at least one pharmacy, although only in Colombo will you find late night and 24-hour pharmacies.

L

LANGUAGE

The main language is Sinhala, the language of the Sinhalese, spoken by around 75 percent of the population. Significant numbers of westernised Sri Lankans in Colombo actually speak English as a first language alongside Sinhala. Anyone involved with tourism will almost certainly speak good English, and you should have few problems communicating. There is no practical incentive to learn any Sinhala except to satisfy yourself. Sinhala speakers generally respond to foreigners' attempts at speaking their language with incomprehension or, at best, polite amusement. The following expressions will raise a gratified smile, but for anything more complicated, stick to English.

hello/welcome/goodbye	**ayubowan**
yes	**oh-uh**
no	**nay**
please	**karuna karala**
thank you	**es-toothy**
sorry	**kana gartui**
excuse me	**sama venna**
How are you?	**Kohomada?**
Good, thanks.	**Honeen innava.**

M

MAPS

The best general map of the island is the Rough Guide map of Sri Lanka (1:500,000), which is extremely detailed, and also printed on indestructible plastic paper. The Survey Department's *Road Atlas of Sri Lanka*, available from many bookshops in the island, has useful road maps and town plans.

MEDIA

Sri Lanka has plenty of English-language publications and radio stations. There are no fewer than five English-language national newspapers (three dailies and two Sunday papers). Two (*The Daily News* and *Sunday Observer*) are indirectly controlled by the government, and so offer a rather biased view of events; better are the independently owned *The Daily Mirror*, *The Island* and *Sunday Times*, though the indifferent journalistic standards, curious style of written English and dense political jargon can make reading any of them a struggle. Foreign newspapers are only rarely available, and then at least a few days out of date; your best bet is to read them online. There is a burgeoning number of English-language monthly magazines as well. The excellent *Travel Sri Lanka* has insightful features on various aspects of the island, while *Travel Lanka* is also worth a look, as is the business-oriented *Lanka Monthly Digest*, which runs some good general-interest articles.

A number of English-language radio stations broadcast out of Colombo (though reception away from the capital is patchy). These mainly serve up a fairly bland diet of Western pop and inane (if sometimes unintentionally comic) chat; the best is TNL Rocks (101.7 FM). The BBC World Service and Voice of America are also widely broadcast. There is almost no locally produced English-language TV, though rooms in many smarter hotels have satellite TV offering the standard range of BBC, CNN and Star sports and movie channels.

MONEY

The Sri Lankan currency is the rupee, abbreviated variously as R, R/, or Rs. Coins come in denominations of Rs. 1, 2, 5 and 10, and 50 and 25 cents. Notes come in denominations of Rs.10, 20, 50, 100, 200 (rare), 500 and 1,000. At the time of writing the exchange rate was around Rs.175 to one British pound, and Rs.110 to one US dollar. Change is usually in short supply except in more up-market establishments – do not expect to pay for a Rs.50 rickshaw ride with a Rs.1000 note, and take the opportunity to break large notes wherever possible.

To guard against the effects of inflation, many smarter hotels and tour operators give prices in dollars or euros, although payment will be expected in rupees, calculated at the day's exchange rate. MasterCard and Visa are widely accepted at top-end places, and most towns around the island now have at least one ATM which accepts foreign MasterCard and Visa credit cards. Travellers' cheques are easily changed at any bank, although it is best to stick to cheques from a major brand (American Express and Thomas Cook are both safe bets) denominated in dollars, sterling or euros.

OPENING TIMES

Government offices and larger businesses usually observe a standard five-day working week from Monday to Friday. Post offices usually open Mon–Sat 8am–6pm, or later at larger branches. Banks generally open Mon–Fri from around 8–9am to 2–3pm. Smaller businesses and shops tend to stay open seven days a week – there is no particular tradition of Sunday closures, although in Muslim areas businesses sometimes shut for all or part of Friday. Most restaurants are open daily from early in the morning until the last customer leaves, although some establishments in Colombo close in the afternoons from around 3–6pm. Some museums, especially those in Colombo, shut on Fridays, or on one other weekday. Buddhist temples tend to be open more or less around the clock; Hindu temples, by contrast, often stay shut between the early morning and late afternoon *pujas*.

P

POLICE

Sri Lankan police are generally friendly and will do their best to be helpful but are not noted for their English-language skills. If you have a problem or need to report a crime, it is best, if possible, to take a Sinhala-speaking local with you to assist with translation. There are tourist police offices in a few towns around the island, though they are usually no better than regular police stations.

POST OFFICES

There are post offices in all towns (and even some villages) across the island, usually open Mon–Sat from around 8am–6pm, or later. Those in larger towns have IDD phone and express mail (known locally as EMS Speed Post) services, as well as free poste restante facilities (ask for mail to be addressed 'c/o The Postmaster, General Post Office, Town' with your surname underlined). If sending a parcel abroad, take the contents unwrapped to the post office for inspection before you wrap them up – larger post offices usually have kiosks selling string, tape and brown paper.

PUBLIC HOLIDAYS

There are no fewer than 24 annual public holidays in Sri Lanka, plus many other festivals during which things grind to a halt. All 12 full-moon days (*poya* days) are Buddhist festivals and public holidays; these occur on the full-moon day of every month, and vary in exact date from year to year. The exact dates of the other public holidays marked with an asterisk also vary from year to year, being calculated according to the Buddhist or Hindu lunar calendar, which means it's largely impossible to predict exact future dates. The Muslim festivals listed below (and marked **) are timed according to local astronomical sightings of phases of the moon and again, the dates given below are for estimated dates in 2011, although these may vary slightly.

Tamil Thai Pongal 14 or 15 January
Independence Day 4 February
Milad un-Nabi** 16 February
Maha Sivarathri One day in Feb/March (2 March 2011)
Good Friday* One day in March/April (22 April 2011)
Sinhalese and Tamil New Year 13 and 14 April
Labour Day 1 May
Eid al-Fitr** 31 August
Eid al-Adha** 6 November
Deepavali Late October/early November (26 Oct 2011)
Christmas Day 25 December

R

RELIGION

The world's four largest religions are all practised in Sri Lanka. The majority of the population (about 70 percent) are Buddhist, while the remainder is more or less equally divided between Hindus, Muslims and Christians. Almost all Sinhalese are Buddhist, while most Tamils are Hindu (though there are also significant numbers of Tamil Christians). Religion remains a dominant cultural force throughout the island in all communities.

T

TELEPHONES

The country code for Sri Lanka is 94; the international access code to dial out of Sri Lanka is 00, followed by the relevant country code.

All Sri Lankan landline numbers have 10 digits, including a three-digit area code. There are few public phone booths on the street in Sri Lanka; it is usually easier to find a 'communications bureau' – there are usually at least a couple of these in any town of note, offering phone, fax and sometimes email facilities, along with photocopying and mobile-phone accessories.

You make your call either from a phone booth or from a phone at the counter and pay the bill at the end: count on around Rs.75 per minute for calls to the UK, North America and Australasia. Most smarter hotels have in-room IDD phones, but rates from these are significantly higher. Local and national calls don't usually cost more than about Rs.10 per minute.

There is good mobile coverage across most parts of the island, even in the north. Alternatively, you can buy a Sri Lankan SIM card for around $10 which gets you a local phone number and allows you to make international calls for as little as Rs.30 per minute; Dialog, Mobitel and Airtel are the largest companies.

TIME ZONES

Sri Lanka's clocks follow Indian Standard Time (IST). This means that Sri Lanka is at Coordinated Universal Time UTC (GMT) + 5½ – 5½ hours ahead of GMT in winter and 4½ hours in summer; 10½ hours ahead of New York in winter and 9½ in summer.

TIPPING AND TAXES

The upmarket hotels and restaurants often add a service charge of 10 percent to their bills, and you might also be hit with a 15 percent GST (Government Service Tax). The resultant 25 percent surcharge on top of published prices can be a nasty surprise when you come to pay the bill, so it is always worth checking menus and hotel rates when you arrive. More downmarket establishments rarely levy either charge. If you think you have been well looked after, a tip of 10 percent or so should suffice.

TOILETS

There are no public toilets in Sri Lanka, although as a foreigner you should not have any problems wandering into the nearest hotel to discreetly avail yourself of the facilities. Almost all toilets are Western-style flush toilets rather than Asian squat toilets, and are usually kept tolerably clean. Toilet paper is almost always provided, though there's no harm in carrying some emergency supplies.

TOURIST INFORMATION

Official sources of tourist information in Sri Lanka are virtually non-existent. There are only two properly set-up tourist information offices, in Colombo (80 Galle Road, Colombo 3, tel: 011-243 7055) and Kandy (Temple Street, by the entrance to the Temple of the Tooth, tel: 081 222 2661). This massive gap is filled by local guesthouse owners and local tour operators. Many guesthouse owners are experts in their area and can tell you all you need to know, as well as arranging car hire, tours and other services. Tour operators can also be found all over the island, especially in Colombo and down the west coast, and can often be valuable sources of information and practical help.

Sri Lanka Tourism (www.srilanka.travel) has several offices around the world:

Australia: 29 Lonsdale St, Braddon, ACT 2612, tel: 02-6230 6002.
Ireland: 59 Ranelagh Rd, Dublin 6, tel: 01-496-9621.
UK: 3rd Floor, 1 Devonshire Square, London EC2M 4WD, tel: 0845-880 6333.
US: 111 Wood Avenue South, Iselin, NJ 08830, tel: 0732-516 9800.

TRANSPORT

Public transport is plentiful and incredibly cheap, but also generally slow and uncomfortable.

Bus. The staple means of transport is by bus; every town of any size on the island has regular services, and there are very few places where the network doesn't reach. Buses are either of two types. Government-run buses (usually big orange rustbuckets) are the cheapest, slowest and most crowded, and tend to stop everywhere and anywhere there is a passenger to be picked up. Private buses come in all sorts of forms: the most basic resemble government-run buses in speed and (lack of) comfort. Faster services (usually signed 'semi-express' or 'express') tend to make more limited stops and to be a bit quicker, at least in theory. Fastest of all are the privately run express minibuses which ply the routes between major cities. These are often twice as fast as the other buses; the interiors are rather cramped, but at least they don't usually get clogged up with standing passengers, as the slower and larger buses do. Fares on all buses are extremely cheap, ranging from as little as Rs.30 per hour of travel on the cheapest buses up to Rs.100 per hour on express minibuses. Advance reservations are virtually unheard of. All larger towns have bus terminals, though it is often possible to flag down buses by the roadside.

Train. Sri Lanka's antiquated railway system offers a charming – if slow way of getting round the island, especially on the scenic hill country line. Fares are dirt cheap – the standard (second-class) fare from Colombo to Kandy, for example, costs little more than a dollar. Most trains consist of basic second- and even more basic third-class carriages; seats in these carriages cannot be reserved, so the chances are that you might end up standing for at least part of the ride. The hill country train also has a so-called 'observation carriage', with large windows and plusher than usual seating. Places in the observation carriage have to be reserved in advance (most easily done at Colombo Fort or Kandy stations) and tend to sell out quickly.

Tuktuk. The Sri Lankan rickshaw, known variously as tuktuks, three-wheelers or (somewhat euphemistically) 'taxis', are the staple means of covering short distances around towns, and can sometimes be useful for covering longer journeys in the country in places where bus services are sketchy. Bargaining is the order of the day, and you should always agree a fare before setting off to avoid arguments, unpleasantness and rip-offs later. Estimating how much a journey should cost is difficult, but as a rough rule of thumb count on Rs.50–60 per kilometre. The longer the journey, the cheaper the per-kilometre rate should be.

Plane. There are regular domestic services from Colombo's Ratmalana airport to Jaffna and Trincomalee; both flights take about an hour and, at a cost of around $150–200 return.

V

VISAS AND ENTRY REQUIREMENTS

Citizens of the UK, Ireland, US, Canada, Australia and New Zealand are given a free 30-day tourist visa on arrival; this can easily be extended to three months at the Department of Immigration in Colombo (fees vary according to nationality).

When you leave Sri Lanka, you are not allowed to export any 'antiques' (classified as anything more than 50 years old) or any animal parts or marine products (including coral and shells) without a licence. If you need a licence, ask at the tourist office in Colombo for details.

W

WEBSITES AND INTERNET ACCESS

Colombo and Kandy have plenty of well-set up internet cafés with broadband connections. However, anywhere which sees a reasonable number of tourists is likely to have places offering internet access, and most top-end hotels also have access. Rates vary from Rs.2 per minute in Colombo and Kandy up to Rs.10 per minute in less well-connected places.

www.srilanka.travel.com Sri Lanka tourism, travel facts and links to destinations and accommodation information.

www.srilankatourism.org General travel information, tourist attractions. calendar of events.

www.fco.gov.uk Safe travel advice.

Recommended Hotels

Sri Lanka boasts a plethora of accommodation in all price ranges, and the following listings represent only a small selection of the very best of what's available. Reservations are pretty much essential at the more upmarket places, while the better budget guesthouses can also get booked up at busy times of the year, so it's always worth phoning a couple of days in advance to make sure of a room. Prices in most places vary according to season and demand; establishments along the west and (to a lesser extent) south coasts generally hike their prices up from November through to April. Rates at many places can be negotiable, especially if business is slow and you're planning on staying for a few days. Rooms in more expensive hotels are usually quoted in dollars, though they are payable in rupees at the daily exchange rate. Many more upmarket places levy a 10 percent service charge and a 15 percent government service tax on top of the basic room rate, adding a nasty twist to the final bill if you're not expecting it.

As a basic guide to prices, we have used the following symbols (for a standard double or twin room in high season):

$$$$$	over $200
$$$$	$100–200
$$$	$60–100
$$	$30–60
$	below $30

COLOMBO

Cinnamon Grand $$$$ *77 Galle Road, tel: 011-243 7437, www. cinnamonhotels.com.* Colombo's grandest hotel, with plenty of five-star glitz and style, although rates are surprisingly affordable rates. In-house facilities include a superb spread of restaurants and the lovely Angsana Spa, while rooms are attractively furnished, and come with great views over downtown Colombo.

Galle Face Hotel $$$$ *Galle Face Green, Colombo 3, tel: 011-254 1010, www.gallefacehotel.com.* Famous old colonial hotel and

Colombo landmark, with lots of period charm and an unrivalled oceanfront setting at the south end of Galle Face Green. Rooms in the old ('Classic') wing are somewhat faded, though they retain a certain old-fashioned aura, while those in the new Regency Wing offer colonial style combined with modern international-standard luxury. There is also an attractive spa and a romantic seafront bar and restaurant.

Havelock Place Bungalow $$$ *6 Havelock Place, Colombo 5, tel: 011-258 5191, www.havelockbungalow.com*. This peaceful, low-key boutique hotel is tucked away in the southern city in a pair of stylishly converted colonial bungalows which combine period character and modern comforts.

Mount Lavinia Hotel $$$$ *Hotel Road, Mount Lavinia, tel: 011-271 1711, www.mountlaviniahotel.com*. Sprawling landmark hotel set on the seafront in the beachside suburb of Mount Lavinia. Built around the 19th-century residence of former British governor Sir Thomas Maitland, the hotel combines period atmosphere with contemporary comforts, while there's also a gorgeous stretch of private beach and an excellent spa. Very popular with foreign wedding parties and honeymooners.

Tintagel $$$$$ *65 Rosmead Place, tel: 011-460 2121, www.paradiseroadhotels.com*. Luxurious boutique hotel occupying the atmospheric colonial mansion which was formerly the family home of the Bandaranaike family, who have provided Sri Lanka with three prime ministers since Independence. Accommodation is in one of ten luxurious suites, while facilities include a picture-perfect little infinity pool and a very chi-chi in-house restaurant and bar.

THE WEST COAST

BERUWALA, ALUTHGAMA AND BENTOTA

Club Villa $$$ *138/15 Galle Road, Bentota, tel: 034-227 5312, www.club-villa.com*. One of the most personable small hotels in Sri

Lanka, set in a beautiful spot at the quiet southern end of Bentota beach and occupying a scatter of intimate, superbly designed colonial-style buildings set around a gorgeous garden running down to the sea.

Hemadan $$ *25 River Avenue, Aluthgama, tel: 034-227 5320, email: hemadan@wow.lk.* The most characterful accommodation in Aluthgama, this appealing little guesthouse has simple but comfortable rooms in a pleasant white building with an attractive garden running down to the Bentota lagoon – a beautiful spot. There is a free boat service over to the quiet stretch of beach opposite if you want to get out onto the sand.

Saman Villas $$$$$ *Aturuwella, Bentota, tel: 034-227 5435, www.samanvilla.com.* Stunningly situated on a bluff high above the ocean with sweeping views up and down the coast, this ultra-chic boutique hotel has luxurious rooms filled with every conceivable mod-con, a gorgeous spa and one of the most spectacular swimming pools in Sri Lanka.

Serendib Hotel $$$$ *Bentota, tel: 034-227 5353, www.serendib leisure.com.* Unpretentious but quietly stylish beachfront resort hotel on one of the nicest stretches of beach in Bentota. Rooms are simple but good value, and the whole atmosphere is pleasantly low-key compared with other nearby resorts – and there is a beautiful spa to dive into if you need to unwind. A very laid-back atmosphere compared to the busier resorts further up the beach.

HIKKADUWA

Amaya Reef $$$$ *400 Galle Road, tel: 091-438 3244, www.amaya resorts.com.* The only top-end hotel in Hikkaduwa itself (though at a very reasonable price), this attractive beachfront establishment is a good example of contemporary Sri Lankan design, with attractive minimalist rooms in muted shades of teak, ochre and white, a good open-air seafront restaurant and large pool.

Neela's $ *634 Galle Road, Narigama, tel: 091-438 3166, email: neelas_sl@hotmail.com.* This long-established guesthouse is one of the friendliest and best-value places to stay in Hikkaduwa, with a fine beachside location, good home-cooking and bright and comfortable modern rooms.

NEGOMBO

Browns Beach Hotel $$$$ *Lewis Place, tel: 031-555 5000, www.aitkenspencehotels.com.* Large and attractive resort hotel which rambles for a considerable distance along the beach, but manages to feel cheerful and surprisingly homely despite its size. There's also a huge pool and plenty of other facilities.

Jetwing Ayurveda Pavilions $$$$ *Porutota Road, tel: 031-487 0764, www.jetwinghotels.com.* Tucked away in the middle of Negombo, this idyllic little hideaway boasts twelve luxurious little villas, each with its own private garden and open-air bathroom, and with expert staff providing a wide range of rejuvenating Ayurveda treatments.

Jetwing Beach $$$$$ *Porutota Road, Negombo, tel: 031-227 3500, www.jetwinghotels.com.* Negombo's most upmarket resort option, with stylish and superbly appointed rooms, excellent food, a pleasant beachfront setting at the quiet north end of the beach and a beautiful pool, part of which winds underneath the hotel itself between strategically placed frangipani trees.

Ranweli Holiday Village $$$$ *Waikal, tel: 031-227 7359, www.ranweli.com.* Affordable and very peaceful eco-resort squeezed in between the ocean and the old Dutch canal 12km (7½ miles) north of Negombo. Accommodation is in a scatter of rustic villas designed to resemble a traditional Sri Lankan village, while activities range from yoga and Ayurveda courses to boat trips and birdwatching.

Silver Sands $ *Lewis Place, tel: 031-222 2880, www.silver-sands.go2lk.com.* Excellent, long-established budget hotel near the southern end of Negombo beach. The atmosphere is friendly and relaxing, with a good little restaurant, a pleasant garden, rooftop balcony, and simple, cheap rooms.

GALLE

Amangalla $$$$$ *10 Church Street, tel: 091-223 3388, www.aman resorts.com.* Occupying the sensitively restored premises of Galle's famous old New Oriental Hotel, this establishment remains wonderfully faithful to the period character of its colonial predecessor, combining old-world colonial chic with the last word in contemporary luxury – a compelling combination, though not cheap it's worth every penny.

Beach Haven $ *65 Lighthouse Street, tel: 091-223 4663, www. beachhaven-galle.com.* This perennially popular guesthouse seems to have been going for ever and continues to pull in visitors thanks to its cheap and comfortable rooms, tasty home cooking and friendly family atmosphere.

Galle Fort Hotel $$$$$ *28 Church Street, tel: 091-223 2870, www.galleforthotel.com.* Stunning hotel set in a magnificently converted old Dutch warehouse – like the nearby Amangalla, it manages to combine colonial charm and contemporary luxury, though at a far more affordable price. It also dishes up some of Sri Lanka's best foreign cuisine, with a predominantly Southeast Asian slant – a pleasant change if you have had one too many rice and curries.

Jetwing Lighthouse $$$$$ *Dadella, tel: 091-222 3744, www. jetwinghotels.com.* Set on a breezy stretch of seafront a couple of kilometres outside Galle, this Geoffrey Bawa-designed hotel is one of the great Sri Lankan architect's defining creations, with a simple, serene exterior, gorgeously designed rooms and splashes of local colour (such as the remarkable wrought-iron staircase depicting the Portuguese invasion of Ceylon). Excellent food and heaps of facilities too.

The Sun House $$$$$ *18 Upper Dickson Road, tel: 091-438 0275, www.thesunhouse.com.* This long-established boutique guesthouse is still one of the nicest places to stay in Sri Lanka, set in a beautiful old 19th-century planter's villa on a hill high above Galle which has masses of period charm as well as memorable cooking. The adjacent Dutch House offers a slightly more upmarket variation on the same theme, with four huge suites in another historic colonial mansion.

UNAWATUNA

Thambapanni Retreat $$$ *Unawatuna Village, tel: 091-223 4588, www.thambapannileisure.com.* Set a few minutes' walk from the beach, up against the lush, jungle-covered flanks of Rumassala (the huge rocky outcrop behind Unawatuna village), this place has more the atmosphere of a rainforest eco-lodge than a beach hotel. Rooms are comfortable, with neo-colonial furnishings and all mod-cons. Offers yoga, meditation and Reiki treatments.

KOGGALA

The Fortress $$$$$ *Koggala, tel: 091-438 9400, www.thefortress. lk.* Striking new five-star resort, designed to resemble a supersized version of one of Galle's old colonial-era Dutch villas, magnificently framed between superbly landscaped grounds, a vast infinity pool and the sea. The luxurious rooms boast all mod-cons, while facilities include a top-notch spa and a string of excellent restaurants, including the fine-dining Wine3, with walls stacked high with international vintages. The Fortress ranks among the most extravagant and expensive hotels on the island.

TANGALLA

Amanwella $$$$$ *Godellawela, Tangalla, tel: 047-224 1333, fax: 047-224 1334, www.amanresorts.com.* Set on one of the south's most beautiful beaches, this sublime hotel offers some of the finest beachfront accommodation anywhere on the island. Rooms are sumptuous little masterpieces of chic modern interior design, and the overall concept is a serenely simple and artfully understated exercise in low-impact contemporary architecture, whose minimalist lines merge gracefully with surrounding palms.

KANDY

Helga's Folly $$$$ *Off Mahamaya Mawatha, tel: 081-447 4314, www.helgasfolly.com.* Sri Lanka's most eccentric hotel, set on a hill high above Kandy. The interior is like an eccentric museum, with brightly coloured rooms stuffed with huge quantities of bric a brac – animal heads, colonial photos, Indonesian puppets and huge candles covered in clumps of dripping wax – while all rooms are individually decorated with colourful murals. The relative lack of facilities (apart from a small swimming pool) – and absence of package tourists – is all part of the allure.

Jetwing Hunas Falls $$$$ *Elkaduwa, 27km north of Kandy, tel: 081-247 6402, www.jetwing.net.* Located 27km (17 miles) north of Kandy in a sublime position, up in the rugged hills of the Knuckles range, this eco-oriented retreat is one of the nicest hotels around Kandy, with comfortable modern facilities, and plenty of walks and wildlife in the surrounding countryside.

Kandy House $$$$$ *Gunnepana, 5km (3 miles) west of Kandy tel: 081-492 1394, www.thekandyhouse.com.* One of the island's most magical boutique hotels, occupying a wonderfully atmospheric old traditional manor house tucked away in peaceful countrtyside 5km (3 miles) from Kandy. Rooms are beautifully furnished in traditional style, and there's good food and a picture-perfect infinity swimming pool in the lovely landscaped gardens.

Sharon Inn $ *59 Saranankara Road, tel: 081-222 2416, www.hotelsharoninn.com.* Neat, modern and very professionally run guesthouse with comfortable rooms, excellent food and superb views over the lake and town from its hillside setting.

THE HILL COUNTRY

ELLA AND BANDARAWELA

Ambiente $$ *2km (1 mile) from Ella Village, tel: 057-222 8867 www.ambiente.lk.* This low-key modern guesthouse is in one of the best locations in Sri Lanka, high on a hilltop above Ella village with superb views over Ella Gap. Rooms are modern and simple, if on the small side, and the food is good, too.

Bandarawela Hotel $$$ *14 Welimada Road, tel: 057-222 2501, www.aitkenspencehotels.com.* Atmospheric colonial-style hotel set in a 19th-century planters' club house. The rambling old wooden building is full of character, and rooms have bags of old-world ambience – all at a very reasonable price.

NUWARA ELIYA

Glendower $$ *Grand Hotel Road, tel: 052-222 2501, email: glendower22@sltnet.lk.* This modest little half-timbered hotel is Nuwara Eliya's cosiest mid-range option, with period touches, attractive wood-floored rooms, a pub-style bar and the excellent *King Prawn* Chinese restaurant *(see page 113)*.

The Hill Club $$$ *Off Grand Hotel Road, tel: 052-222 2653, www.hillclubsrilanka.net.* Set in a rugged old granite and half-timbered building close to the town centre, this famous hotel offers a real taste of colonial Ceylon. The time-warped interior includes a musty billiards room, library and an atmospheric restaurant *(see page 113)*, plus assorted stuffed stags' heads, cracked leather furniture and shelves of yellowing novels. Accommodation is in neat, slightly chintzy rooms with creaking wooden floors – like a rather superior British B&B.

Heritance Tea Factory $$$$$ *Kandapola, tel 052-222 9600, www.aitkenspencehotels.com.* Stunning hotel set in an ingeniously converted tea factory – the factory exterior has been perfectly preserved, but the interior has been magically transformed into a sleek modern five-star. The stylish design combines futuristic architectural lines with lots of old tea-making memorabilia and machines, while the setting high up in the hills and surrounded by miles of tea plantation – is another major attraction.

Jetwing St Andrews $$$$ *10 St Andrew's Drive, tel: 052-222 3031, www.jetwinghotels.com.* Nuwara Eliya's smartest hotel, occupying a beautiful colonial country club surrounded by graceful lawns running down to the golf course. The oak-panelled bar and restaurant are pure Edwardian period pieces, while rooms are cosy (some with four-poster beds) and comfortable.

ANURADHAPURA

Tissawewa Grand $$$ *Old Town, tel: 025-222 2299, www.quick shaws.com*. The most memorable place to stay in Anuradhapura, This atmospheric old colonial rest house (recently refurbished and upgraded) has lots of period charm and an unbeatable location right at the heart of the old ruined city (though this also means that no alcohol is served).

DAMBULLA

Heritance Kandalama $$$$$ *Kandalama Lake, 10km (6 miles) from Dambulla, tel: 066-555 5000, www.aitkenspencehotels.com*. One of Sri Lanka's most original hotels, this Bawa-designed establishment presents the ultimate marriage of architecture and nature, clinging to the side of a huge rocky outcrop and almost completely buried by layers of tropical vegetation. Stunning views of Sigiriya and the Kandalama lake, plush rooms, and one of the island's most spectacular swimming pools all add to the allure.

SIGIRIYA

Jetwing Vil Uyana $$$$$ *3km (2 miles) east of Inamaluwa Junction, tel: 066-492 3584, www.jetwinghotels.com*. Half hotel and half nature reserve, Vil Uyana sits amidst a beautiful artificial wetland created using ancient Sri Lankan irrigation techniques. Accommodation is in sumptuous villas scattered amidst wildlife-rich areas of marshland, paddy fields, forest and around the central lake, with facilities including a stunning infinity pool plus superb restaurant and spa.

HABARANA

Cinnamon Lodge $$$$ *Habarana Village, tel: 066-227 0011, www.johnkeellshotels.com.* Located in the crossroads town of Habarana, and conveniently placed for day trips to all the Cultural Triangle's major sites (if you bring your own car), this rustic, low-key hotel has plush accommodation in individual villas scattered around extensive and beautiful tree-shaded grounds.

POLONNARUWA

Rest House $$$ *Polonnaruwa, tel: 027-222 2299, www.ceylon hotels.lk.* This venerable old rest house retains much of its old-fashioned charm, despite recent refurbishments, while the superb location, perched on the edge of the great Parakrama Samudra lake, can't be beaten.

THE EAST COAST

TRINCOMALEE

Nilaveli Beach Hotel $$$ *Nilaveli, tel: 026-223 2295, www.tangerinehotels.com.* Unpretentious, long-established resort hotel right on Nilaveli beach opposite Pigeon Island, with a range of comfortable rooms of varying prices and standards and a decent range of facilities.

ARUGAM BAY

Hideaway $ *Arugam Bay, tel: 063-224 8259.* Attractive and excellent-value small guesthouse set a few minutes inland from the beach. Rooms are simple but attractively furnished, while the owner's striking photos of elephants from nearby Lahugala National Park decorate the corridors and verandah.

Rocco's Hotel $$ *Arugam Bay, tel: 077-664 2991.* Located midway along the bay, this small hotel offers comfortable rooms. The open bar/restaurant is an excellent place to chill out.

INDEX

Berlitz pocket guide

Sri Lanka

Second Edition 2011

Written by Gavin Thomas
Edited by Paula Soper
Series Editor: Tom Stainer

Photography credits
All images Sylvaine Poitau/APA except
Ravindralal Anthonis 72
Mary Evans 19, 20
David Henley/APA 1, 36, 42, 45, 46, 61, 82, 83, 86, 102, 108
Istockphoto 3ML, 95
Marcus Wilson-Smith/APA 2BR, 3BL, 18, 35, 41, 58, 59, 81, 85, 104
Popperfoto/Alamy 22

Cover picture: 4Corners Images

Every effort has been made to provide accurate information in this publication, but changes are inevitable. The publisher cannot be responsible for any resulting loss, inconvenience or injury.

Contact us

At Berlitz we strive to keep our guides as accurate and up to date as possible, but if you find anything that has changed, or if you have any suggestions on ways to improve this guide, then we would be delighted to hear from you.

Berlitz Publishing, PO Box 7910, London SE1 1WE, England.
email: berlitz@apaguide.co.uk
www.berlitzpublishing.com